T0147078

Priority of Prayer

Dr. B. L. Worsham, Th.D.

WESTBOW
PRESS®
A DIVISION OF THOMAS NELSON
& ZONDERVAN

Copyright © 2022 Dr. B. L. Worsham, Th.D.

All rights reserved. No part of this book may be used or reproduced by any means, graphic, electronic, or mechanical, including photocopying, recording, taping or by any information storage retrieval system without the written permission of the author except in the case of brief quotations embodied in critical articles and reviews.

This book is a work of non-fiction. Unless otherwise noted, the author and the publisher make no explicit guarantees as to the accuracy of the information contained in this book and in some cases, names of people and places have been altered to protect their privacy.

WestBow Press books may be ordered through booksellers or by contacting:

WestBow Press
A Division of Thomas Nelson & Zondervan
1663 Liberty Drive
Bloomington, IN 47403
www.westbowpress.com
844-714-3454

Because of the dynamic nature of the Internet, any web addresses or links contained in this book may have changed since publication and may no longer be valid. The views expressed in this work are solely those of the author and do not necessarily reflect the views of the publisher, and the publisher hereby disclaims any responsibility for them.

Any people depicted in stock imagery provided by Getty Images are models, and such images are being used for illustrative purposes only. Certain stock imagery © Getty Images.

The Authorized (King James) Version of the Bible ('the KJV'), the rights in which are vested in the Crown in the United Kingdom, is reproduced here by permission of the Crown's patentee, Cambridge University Press. The Cambridge KJV text including paragraphing, is reproduced here by permission of Cambridge University Press.

ISBN: 978-1-6642-6677-3 (sc)
ISBN: 978-1-6642-6679-7 (hc)
ISBN: 978-1-6642-6678-0 (e)

Library of Congress Control Number: 2022909154

Print information available on the last page.

WestBow Press rev. date: 6/23/2022

Dedication Page

To my wife Doris Worsham who worked tirelessly to not only type each page, but to pray and encourage me "to keep on, keeping on" thank you my love. Without you there would be no book, and to our children, Pamela and her husband William Parker for their love and support, and technical help with publishing our book.

2020, A Hard Year

"...Truly God is good..." (Psalm 73:1)!

A hard year2020! Trouble for millions, universal illness; wide-spread deaths: "My steps have well-nigh slipped" (Psalm 73:2). We witnessed- corona virus-ravage our nation and the entire world. It is within God's permissive will, we believe, that He has allowed the Pandemic to speak to all His creation. The principles and teachings of our fundamental faith led us to this conclusion. But the same faith answers in God's grace and mercy toward us:

God's redemptive answer!

> *"If my people...shall humble themselves; and pray; and seek my face, And turn from their wicked ways, them will I hear from heaven and will forgive their sin and will heal their land" (2 Chronicles 7:14).*

Yet so many scoff at God's voice and turn a deaf ear toward our Father's perfect solution. Let us learn, if we follow the world's wealth; search for purpose and fulfilment in the changing economies of society, and gage success by money, we will fail! Remember we consist of two parts; a dichotomy; body (mortal) and soul (immortal). Mostly we feed our bodies and starve our souls! Beloved, we must all die—what then?

Know, when the corona virus relents, worse will follow in this world. "For all-the-day long have I been plagued and chastened every morning" (Psalm 73:14). The Word of God has spoken. We have the answer before us. "...they that are far from thee shall perish...But it is good for me to draw near to God" (Psalm 73:27-28). Dear friend, let us pray... and every soul declare "... I have put my trust in the Lord God..." Psalm 73:28).

"Truly, God is good" (Psalm 73: 1).

God bless you!

A Better Testament

"Wherefore He is able also to save them to the uttermost
that come unto God by Him, seeing that he ever lives
to make intercession for them" (Hebrews 7:25).

This has been our prayer for many days –that God would grant, in Jesus' name–relenting grace, concerning this worldwide "plague of Corona Virus!" We know that you Lord, are in control of all things. That you determine or permit whatever occurs among your creation. We know that you created man with self-determination. And we are persuaded that all, including your people, have decided to turn to our own ways and grossly sin in your sight.

Because of our flagrant iniquity, we believe you have spoken to us in a manner that has affected every human on the earth. Millions have died; millions are suffering, and the economies of the world are devastated. The brightest, most able, most educated are searching for the answer; all are failing! But at last, many are looking up to you; realizing that you have permitted this terrible sickness to invade the world because of our great sinfulness!

Father, we confess! We have sinned! Spiritually, physically, mentally, and emotionally we have sinned! We have taken the perfect world which you created and turned it into chaos. Even our beautiful country, the land of the free and the home of the brave, is in constant conflict all because of sin! We repent and name our unrighteous acts one by one. We pray for your mercy, love, and forgiveness. We believe: "Draw near to God and He will draw near to you…" (James 4:8).

We thank you Father, Son, and Holy Spirit, that you give us hope. We believe prayer heals. We believe, "The effectual fervent prayer of a righteous man availeth much" (James 5:16). And we testify again that,

"By so much was Jesus made a surety of a better Testament" (Hebrews 7:22).

God bless you!

A Christmas Prayer

"In the beginning was the word, and the word was
with God, and the word was God" (John 1:1).

Jesus Christ the "Divinely anointed of God!" "Son of God!" "Co-equal with God" (John 1:1-14)!

You are the giver of eternal life, (John 17:2), Savior of believers (Ephesians 2:8-10), Creator and Judge of all life here and hereafter (Isaiah 40:28), and rewarder of every believing soul (Acts 13:39); we come with bended knee, and joyful hearts to celebrate your incarnation-Christmas!

This time of sacredness is set apart from all other days, to celebrate the fullness of time when You graced the earth to show us the way of salvation. We lift our hands, our souls, and our prayers to thank You: for giving Your life so that whosoever will believe in You may live in eternity.

We pray that Your kingdom will come, and Your will shall be done on earth as it is in heaven. We pray for the time when "…peace on earth, good will to men" (Luke 2:14), will be the first wish and act of every human. We pray that the Holy Spirit will enter the hearts of all leaders of all lands and wars and strife will cease.

We pray for forgiveness for ourselves, our families, our nation of America, and every lost soul. Lord, we rejoice where You have said, … "Surely I come quickly," and in Jesus' name we repeat

"—Amen. Even so, come, Lord Jesus" (Revelation 22:20)

God bless you!

A Prayer of Promise

"My praise shall be to thee in the great congregation: I will pay my vows before them that fear Him." (Psalm 22:25)

This is a prayer of promise! It is a time of comfort when we can come before the Lord, and instead of asking Him for our needs, simply praise Him for grace and mercy. God is good! He never forsakes or deserts us. He sees us when we exhibit thoughts and words that are sinful totally unbecoming to a Christian and He loves us despite this.

He does so because He cares! He loves us with an eternal agape. All who seek the Lord and follow His ways, "your heart shall live forever" (Psalm 22:26). Those who ask God for direction shall not go astray. They find that "...He is the governor among the nations" (Psalm 22:28). He is "omnipotent" (almighty), "omniscient" (all knowing), and "omnipresent" (everywhere). Therefore, our heavenly Father is almighty, to deliver us from harm; possesses all knowledge, to answer every prayer; and is with us, each moment, to hear and know our circumstances

More than that, God delights to fill our lives with good and righteous things. When we approach His throne of grace in Jesus' name and under the guidance of the Holy Spirit, He hears and answers! When we have prayed in His will, we know He will grant our petition or give an answer that is better than we anticipated.

God has ordained prayer as our greatest connection with Him! In prayer we speak directly with God in Jesus's name. After salvation, this is our most marvelous privilege! Therefore, pray, but pray wisely "...for He is Lord of Lords, and King of Kings: And they that are with Him are called, and chosen, and faithful" (Revelation 17:14).

Let us pray: "...I will pay my vows before them that fear Him" (Psalm 22:25).

God bless you!

A Sower Went Out to Sow

Jesus said, "...Behold a Sower went forth to sow..." (*Matthew* 13:3):

Here is a wonderful thing, a special work; a precious type of seed; an expansive field in which to sow, and a blessing attached to every seed. All who will sow can be employed in this "seed-sowing"! And no person is excluded!

It is true that God equipped some in special ways: The Bible states: "He gave some, apostles; some, prophets; some, evangelists; some, pastors and teachers; for the perfecting of the saints..." (Ephesians 4:11-12). These people are called for a special purpose! But you, whoever you are and whatever your craft, vocation, avocation, occupation, or labor you are not left out! Yours is the most important sowing of all and when neglected, the greatest loss of all! Where do we arrive at this starling idea? From the Bible!

"...ye shall receive power, after that the Holy Ghost is come upon you: and you shall be witnesses unto me both in Jerusalem, in Judaea, in Samaria, and unto the uttermost part of the earth" (Acts 1:8). Surly not, you may say, I have no training you say! But the promise is, "Ye shall receive power..." (Acts 1:8)! I would not know what to say! But beloved, it is a commandment. "...Ye shall be witnesses unto Me..." (Acts 1:8). These are simply your excuses. I don't travel the earth! I only see the grocers, the schoolteacher, my employer, the people at work, or at church, my family, and my friends they are all I see! My Lord doesn't command any more of you than these! They are your uttermost part of the earth. And these are the people God holds you responsible for. You have opportunity to speak to them about Jesus most often!

What shall I say? you ask. Very simply tell them what God has done for you your family your life and your soul! You will see in eternity, the result of your prayers when you

"…went forth to sow!" (Matthew 13:3)

God bless you!

A Special Gift

"By humility and the fear of the Lord are riches,
and honor, and life" (Proverbs 22:4).

I was gifted by a Pastor friend with a volume of forgotten Puritan Prayers. The Puritan Movement was a religious movement of Protestants that surfaced in the sixteen and seventeen centuries, in England. Their influence included the preaching of Charles Haddon Spurgeon himself a Baptist Icon (1834-1892).

I take the liberty of sharing one of their prayers. It speaks to the subject: "Man's Greatest End"!

> *"There is one thing that deserves my greatest care, that I may answer the greatest end for which I am made to glorify thee who hast given me being, and to do all the good I can for my fellow man; verily, life is not worth having if it be not improved for this noble purpose.*
>
> *How little is this the thought of mankind! Most men live for themselves, without much or any regard for thy glory; they earnestly desire and eagerly pursue the riches, honors, pleasures, of this life, as if they supposed that wealth, greatness, merriment, could make their immortal souls happy. Help me know continually that there can be no true happiness, no fulfilling of thy Purpose for me, apart from a life lived in and for the son of thy love."* [1]

Praise the Lord that these godly saints, though persecuted, could reach God with such grace, and leave a trail for us to follow!

God bless you!

---

[1] Arthur Bennett, first published in 1975, The Valley of Vision page 22

A Vow to God

"Praise waits for thee, O God, in Sion. And unto thee
shall the vow be performed" (Psalms 65:1).

We refer to our words as promises, or more loosely, as good intentions. To some they are nothing more than, passing fancies, easily spoken, quickly forgotten. This soon becomes habitual; a hard habit to break, and too often a negative impact upon our character. A word to the wise: Do not be too quick to promise, nor too prone to break your word: Others will grow to doubt you! People will say, "you can't believe a word that person says." Sometimes said of political speeches!

Webster's New World Thesaurus explains the word "promise" as meaning: to give one's word; to declare; to pledge, to guarantee. The opposite: to deceive; to deny; break faith. This is a very serious business! The Bible looks upon a promise made to God as a "vow": much stricter than our causal word!

The Bible commands: "Be not rash with thy mouth and let not thine heart be hasty to utter anything before God: For God is in heaven, and thou upon earth: therefore, let thy words be few. When thou vowest a vow unto God, delay not to pay it; for He has no pleasure in fools: pay that which thou hast vowed. Better is it that thou should not vow, than that thou vow and not pay. Suffer not thy mouth to cause thy flesh to sin" (Ecclesiastes 5:2,4-6).

Let us vow together now, with full knowledge, and in total sincerity; that we beseech God, in Jesus's name, for a great awakening in 2022 in our local areas; and in our United States of American. We are convinced there is no other way but through prayer that revival can come to our world. Beloved, vow to pray daily with us, and all our churches! Our text promises: "Praise waits for thee O God, in Sion. And unto thee shall the vow be performed" (Psalms 65:1).

God bless you!

A Work for You

"And the Lord God took the man (Adam) and put him into the garden of Eden to dress it and to keep it" (Genesis 2:15).

Here is the first work ordained by God. A purpose never to be ashamed of and this is the time and season (September) when we honor this word from God, "Labor Day."

Mankind was not created to idle away his God given life; he was mean to work. He/she was given the innate skills to engage in the several works involved in dressing and keeping the earth, Genesis 2:15. God has a work, a plan, for each of us to do, that will fulfill our desire and provide our needs. When we pray and receive salvation, through faith in Jesus Christ that waits for all, by God grace; we will find our life's work. The Holy Spirit will lead us, educate us, equip us, and provide us with our special vocation. That work will not be a labor to us, it will be a pleasure.

My great grandfather was such a man. He loved work. He was a farmer. He owned one hundred acres which he plowed and planted with one mule and much prayer. Today he might be labeled a workaholic. When the moon was full, he would plow all day, stop, sleep a few hours, then he would, go back into the field and plow for several hours by the moonlight. He never complained, he loved work, he loved the land and he loved God. Grandpa knew if he worked hard, God would provide. This is the principle upon which America was built, trust God and work. Beloved it is still the plan for a successful life.

God has a work for you. Trust Him. The Holy Spirit will lead you when you pray and ask him.

God bless you!

Agape

"...God is Love" (1 John 4:8)

The love of God toward his people is "Agape"! Here is the word that expresses the essence, the divine and eternal joy, that God has for humanity! It describes the majesty, the unsearchable greatness of the love that our Father has for you and me.

The Apostle Paul extends all his spiritual integrity when he speaks of "the Preeminence of Love" in chapter thirteen of First Corinthians. He equates this love to "charity" which is "spiritual love." He says, "And though I have the gift of prophecy... and understand all mysteries, and all knowledge, I have all faith, so that I could remove mountains, and I have not charity, (love) I am nothing" (1 Corinthians 13:2).

If a person remains stone- hearted, and emotionally frozen he will never know "love given," nor "love received"!

The one who remains void of God's love will truly exist as a barren fig tree. (Luke13:7) But our Father God has promised: "I will give them one heart, and I will put a new spirit within you, and I will take the stony heart out of their flesh and will give them a heart of flesh ... and they shall be my people, and I will be their God." (Ezekiel 11: 19-20).

When mankind has received salvation, "For by grace are ye saved through faith... it is the gift of God (Ephesians 2:8). He will become capable of true love! He will be a "newborn" child of God, with the full measure of the Holy Spirit inside him; and he can experience the surpassing love of God, and for his brother-man! The unconverted, worldly man does not know what this love is.

> "Many a man with his life out of tune
> All battered and bruised with pain
> Is auctioned cheap to a thoughtless crowd

Much like an old violin,
But Jesu comes — and the (madding) crowd
Can never quite understand,
The worth of a soul, and the change that's made,
By the touch of the master's hand." By Myra Brooks Welch

"…God is Love" (1 John 4:8).

God bless you!

All Done in Jesus's Name

"And whatever you do in word or deed do all in the name of the Lord Jesus, giving thanks to God and the Father by Him" (Colossians 3:17).

Let us begin each day by looking our best! The better we look the better we feel. Whatever we are to encounter—we should always face it with the best persona we have. This may be "dressing-up for the day." If we practice, each morning, it soon becomes our daily habit to present our "best self" to the world every day! Remember, a good person practices a thing till they seldom get it wrong: an excellent person practices a thing until they "cannot" get it wrong. We must decide which we want to be good or excellent!

And there is more, there is the most important ingredient of all Prayer! "My voice you shall hear in the morning, O Lord; in the morning will I direct my prayer unto thee and will look up" (Psalm 5:3). "For the eyes of the Lord are over the righteous, and His ears are open unto their prayers" (1 Peter 3:12). Can we say this in enough ways to convince the doubters? God grant that we may, so, once again; "...the effectual fervent prayer of a righteous man availeth much" (James 5:16. Beloved, prayer changes things! Prayer guides us! Prayer shapes our lives! Prayer allows us to be the best we can be!

When you dress yourself for each day, do not neglect to also dress your heart and soul to successfully deal with every circumstance! Put off the garments of wrath, anger, revenge, and dark thoughts. Instead ask God to fill you with, Things that are true; honest; just; lovely; of good report; virtue; praise (Philippians 4:8).

One of my mother's keepsakes:

> *"The day was long, the burdens I had borne,*
> *Seemed heavier than I could no longer bear,*
> *And then it lifted—but I did not know,*
> *Someone had knelt in prayer."*

Begin each day with joy, "And whatever you do in word or deed, do all in the name of the Lord Jesus, giving thanks to God and the Father, by Him" (Colossians 3:17).

God bless you!

Ask, Seek, Knock

"For everyone that asks receives, and he that seeks finds, and to him that knocks it shall be opened" (Matthew 7:8).

Beloved, have you prayed today? Did you thank God for a good night's rest? Did you praise Him for the day ahead? For the physical ability to embrace whatever should be your challenge with confidence because, "...with God all things are possible" (Matthew 19:26).

Do not become too preoccupied to pray. You are rushed pressed for time facing some critical decision. Brother, you have time to shave, to dress, to eat, remember whatever the day has in store, you will need your strength! However, if this is all you take with you to face your challenge, you are only half a person, your other half; your spiritual-half; your eternal-half, you have neglected if you have not talked to God in Jesus's name.

My friend here is your answer. Today, will require solving problems; the decisions that may impact many days to come, how can you know? You cannot! Only God knows the future and He alone can supply you with the answers. Trust Him, believe Him; follow His leading, and thank Him for it!

This is the work of the Holy Spirit! The Spirit called "Christ-in-you." The spirit you received when you believed in Jesus and were saved. Jesus promised: "I will never leave nor forsake thee" (Hebrews 13:5). And He will guide you safely through any situation you face. Jesus said, "He, the spirit of truth will guide you into all truth; for he will not speak of Himself; but whatever He will hear, that shall He speak, and He will show you things to come. He shall glorify Me (Jesus): for He shall receive of Mine and shall show it unto you" (John 16:13-14).

Beloved, have you prayed today? Have you strengthened both body and soul (physical and spiritual)! If so, you are fully prepared to face this day. Jesus has promised the Christian

"...ask and receive; seek and find; knock and it shall be opened" (Matthew 7:8).

God bless you!

Attention! Youth

"…He being dead yet speaketh." (Hebrew 11:4)

Attention youth! This is for you! Have you felt God's calling to a life of service in the gospel ministry? Especially preaching? I introduce you to C.H. Spurgeon: "The Prince of Preachers," known by thousands—you should know him also! Following is his account of his first sermon, at age fourteen!

By C. H. Spurgeon, "First Sermon"

"We set off along Newmarket Road (England) with a gentleman some years our senior. We expressed our hope that he would feel the presence of God while preaching. He assured us that he had never preached in his life, he was looking to his young friend, Mr. Spurgeon for that. This was a new situation; I could only reply that I was quite unprepared. But there would be no sermon unless I preached. I committed to do my best. After lifting my soul to God, it seemed I could surely tell a few poor cottagers of the love of Jesus. Praying for divine help, I resolved to try. My text would be, "Unto you, therefore, which believe, He is precious." I trusted the Lord to open my mouth. It seemed a serious trial, but depending upon the Holy Spirit, I would tell out the story of the cross.

We entered a cottage where a few farm laborers and their wives were gathered. We sang, prayed, and read the scripture—then came our first sermon. It was not half such a task as we had feared, we were glad to see our way to a fair conclusion. We had not broken down nor stopped short in the middle. We pronounced the benediction and began a dialog which enlarged into a warm friendly talk. "How old are you?" was the leading question. "Under sixteen, was a lady's rejoinder."[2]

---

[2] C. H. Spurgeon First Sermon 1866 Unity in Christ, (ww.w.spurgeon.org)

Spurgeon lived to preach hundreds of great sermons! Look him up! Pray thankfully that he will inspire you! Teach you! Show you how to preach!

… "He being dead yet speaketh" (Hebrew 11:4).

God bless you!

Back for the Future

Excerpts from: Dr. Carrey Froelich (San Jacinto Association)

<u>Seek the Lord</u>. Begin by giving your full attention to the Lord. Ask the Holy Spirit, to guide you.

2 Chronicles 7:14 The Lord said, "If my people shall humble themselves, and pray and seek my face and turn from their wicked ways, then will I hear from heaven and forgive their sin and heal their land."

Isaiah 55:6 "Seek the Lord while he may be found; call upon him for he will abundantly pardon."

Matthew 6:33 "But seek first the kingdom of God and his righteousness, and all these things will be added to you."

<u>Repent</u>. Roman 3:23 "All have sinned and fall short of the glory of God." Ask the Holy Spirit to help you.

2 Chronicles 6:36 "If they sin against you-if they repent with all their mind and with all their heart—then hear from heaven and forgive your people."

Ezekiel 18:30 "Repent, lest iniquity be your ruin, and make yourselves a new heart and a new spirit!"

<u>Intercede</u>. Pray for one another Intercede for their needs among the churches.

2 Thessalonians 3:1 "Finally brothers, pray for us that the word of the Lord may speed ahead and be honored, and that we may be delivered from wicked and evil men. The Lord is faithful, he will establish you and guard you against the evil one."

Pray for unity of believers and for the power of the Holy Spirit to fill all of us.

Pray for pastors of our churches: for the filling of the Holy Spirit of God.
Pray for all church Leaders.
Pray for church members to use their God given gifts in his church.
Pray for those who do not have a personal relationship with Jesus Christ.
Pray for <u>H</u>EART *receptivity*
Pray for <u>E</u>YES *to be opened*
Pray for the <u>A</u>TTITUDE OF GOD *toward sin*
Pray for <u>R</u>EALEASE *to believe*
Pray for <u>T</u>RANSFORMED *lives*

<u>Personal Intercession</u>. Identify areas of need in your life. Thank God for prayer![3]

God bless you!

---

[3] Edited by Dr. B. L. Worsham, permission granted by (<u>careydfoelich@gmail. com</u>) all Scripture is from NKJV www.biblegateway.com

Behold! the Holy Spirit

"...If I depart, I will send Him, (Holy Spirit) unto you" (John 16:7).

The most neglected; least preached; the one mentioned last in prayer is God, the Holy Spirit! Yet the Bible tells, (John 16:7-15), the believer must depend upon the Holy Spirit in learning the truth of Jesus Christ: "Which things also we speak, not in the words which men's wisdom teaches, but which the Holy Ghost teacheth, comparing spiritual things with spiritual" (I Corinthians 2;13). In other words, we know little about God's will for our Christian life! Our spiritual growth is progressive! As we pray, study, hear, we must depend upon the Spirit of God to convict and convince us what is God's truth!

As we go before God in prayer, we must be sensitive to the voice, the impression, the feeling that we receive from the Holy Spirit. "All things that the Father has are Mine: Therefore, said I, that He shall take of Mine, and show it unto you" (John 16:15). And He will! Therefore, I maintain: A Christian can never sin, successfully! The Holy Spirit will not let you! He will remind you over and again, that thought, word or deed you participate in is not pleasing to God, it is sin! The Spirit will continue to present this fact to you, until you repent and ask forgiveness in Jesus's name.

We receive the Holy Spirit (Christ in you) when we are saved. And when He is come, He convicts us of sin; he assures us of forgiveness; He guides our life into all God's truths! We should be aware of how we treat the Holy Spirit. He gives us eternal security! "All manner of sin and blasphemy shall be forgiven unto men: but the blasphemy against the Holy Ghost shall not be forgiven unto men" (Matthew 12:31).

Beloved, make sure you do not ignore the Holy Spirit as you as you pray. He will show you how to pray! "...there is but one God" (I Corinthians 8:6).

Three in one Father, Son, and Holy Spirit.

God bless you!

Billy, Teaching Us to Pray

"...Lord, teach us to pray... (Luke 11: 1)!

Christ taught me when I was fourteen years of age! I had formed my first gospel quartet. We sang daily on radio station KDET, Center, Texas. At times, the local churches would ask us to come and sing at their services. On one such occasion, there was a boy in attendance who we will call, "Billy."

This church was about ten miles out in the deep woods, on a dirt road—a small building, a small congregation! To my surprise "Billy" was there! He did not play football, and he was not on the school basketball team. He rode the bus to school, and on rainy days came in muddy and wet. He was one of those kids who was, "just there"! He was ignored!

Our quartet sang our part and took our seat. There was some preaching—I did not pay much attention: I was thinking about how well we had sounded! Several prayed, and then another voice picked up the praying, and got my attention—it was "Billy"! I was astounded! He sounded like a seasoned preacher, like a prophet. The building did not shake, but I did! I will never forget how Christ was teaching me!

I knew he meant what he said by the earnest sound of his voice! And I knew Jesus heard him because of the faith in his heart! I also realized that "Billy" knew how to pray, and I did not! Suddenly I understood what that disciple meant: "...Lord teaches us to pray..." (Luke 11;1)! I looked around: The entire group was moved by "Billy's" prayer!

The reason many will not pray is because they are not taught! No "family altar" in the home, no praying around the "family circle"! Some are like my quartet—we came mostly to show how great we could sing:

"Billy" came and taught me how to pray! Have we learned?

God bless you!

Bless His Holy Name

"Bless the Lord, O my soul; and all that is within me" (Psalm 103:1

Dear Christian, the past year has been given to "prayer- preparation," the need for personal prayer, God's answer to my prayer, what the Bible tells us about the "how-to" of earnest praying!

Now it is time to make daily prayer a part of our life! If we believe with all our heart that Jesus hears, and Jesus cares, and Jesus intercedes for us, individually! If there is no doubt in our mind, nor faltering in our faith, that the blessed Holy Spirit assists our effort to pray, rightly, when we lift our praise and requests before our heavenly Father!

If we have selected a special time and place, designated it as our prayer closet where we meet with our God on a regular basis! If we have set aside a time to read the Bible every day, if we are convinced that we are in touch with our Lord, then let us go further! Let us never doubt nor fear failure again! Let us covenant with God! Let us, like Moses, strike the "Red Sea" with our "rod of faith" and expect it to open unto us! Beloved, let us not falter, but live by faith and speak.

"As for me, I will call upon God, and the Lord shall save me! Evening, and morning, and at noon, will I pray, and cry aloud: and he shall hear my voice. (Let this be our assurance) He hath delivered my soul in peace from the battle that was against me: for there were many with them. God shall hear and afflict them" (Psalm 55:16-19). In prosperity or in poverty, let my testimony be: "... His mercy is everlasting; and His truth endures to all generations" (Psalm 100:5). And let it be that every thought of our lips says, "Bless the Lord, O my soul: and all that is within me bless His Holy Name" (Psalm 103:1)!

God bless you!

Building Our Soul

"Except the Lord build the house, they labor in
vain that build it: except the Lord keep the city, the
watchman waketh but in vain." (Psalm 127:1)

We take our text to mean that the "house" we are building is our own Christian soul. Never forget Christ has saved your soul "by grace, through faith" (Ephesians 2:8); but your growth into the Christian lifestyle that is what you develop yourself into, will depend upon the spiritual food you feed yourself or fail to. Jesus has given to us, a "sound mind" and for some things we must take responsibility.

Long ago Joshua said, "Choose you this day whom you will serve as for me and my house, we will serve the Lord" (Joshua 24:15). His mind was made-up ahead of time, his goal is set forth in advance, and his vow is spoken to God even before he met the troubles and temptations of life. It is not enough to wait until sin is at the door to decide what you will do spiritually. You need to have a made-up mind already! So, go ahead, make the commitment to yourself and before God. It will give you strength when you face the devil, which you will! Jesus has warned, "These things I have spoken unto you, that in Me you might have peace; in the world you shall have tribulation: but be of good cheer; I have overcome the world" (John 16:33).

Now we must pay close attention to Jesus when He declares, "You are my friends, if you do whatsoever, I command you" (John 15:14). To know the words, then is not enough. The Bible says, "He that keeps His commandments dwells (lives) in Him" (1 John 3:24). We may yet find ourselves laboring in vain. Thankfully, Jesus tells us: "Grow in grace (underserved love), and in the knowledge (revealed obedience) of our Lord and Savior Jesus Christ" (2 Peter 3:18). Now we are not building in vain.

The answer to all the foregoing is prayer! Direct communication with God; constant praying in Jesus's name will fulfill your life, answer every question, and draw you closer to your heavenly Father.

God bless you,

By Grace Alone

"But grow in Grace, and in the knowledge of our Lord..." (2 Peter 3:18).

When we believe in Jesus Christ, confess Him with our lips, and pray for salvation, He saves us at that moment! He writes our name in the "Lamb's Book of Life" We will not be lost, we are elected, for heaven, and Christ will receive us there when we leave this earth through death.

Now we are redeemed, by God's Grace and our faith in Jesus, the question arises how faithful are we? We are commanded: "...Grow in Grace and the knowledge of our Lord and Savior Jesus Christ..." (2 Peter 3:18). How do we grow? By attending God's church regularly! By reading God' Bible each day! And by daily prayer!

At church we hear the Pastor and the Bible school teacher explain God's word. Reading the Bible, we experience God speaking to our heart and mind. In prayer we find ourselves talking directly to our heavenly Father, in the name of Jesus Christ, and during these activities, we will, "...Grow in Grace and knowledge of our Lord Jesus Christ..." (2 Peter3:18).

These things may seem strange to us, if they are new to our lifestyle but Christ does not require of us the thing we cannot do! Soon we are accustomed and have found our favorite seat in the preaching service. Soon, we have cleared the dust from the family Bible, and enjoy the words of life that it contains. And sooner than you think, you are pouring out your heart, your life, your successes, your failure even your sins to God in prayer!

If praying is new to you, you may run out of what to say at first. But you will grow and find more and more to thank God for, to praise Him for, to ask Him for, and to receive from Him! That is because you are growing in your personal relationship with the Lord who loves you, and He is blessing your life!

God bless you!

Casting Stones

"He that is without sin among you, let him first cast a stone" (John 8:7)

The Lost! Some are oblivious! But all are separated from God! In body, soul, and mind by love of sin; drug addiction, refusal of religious practices, immoral living, and mockery toward Jesus Christ.

These souls are easily identified and avoided by most Christians. They may be shunned by believers because they congregate in sinful environments and find their comforts among those much like themselves.

What shall we do about these lost ones? Ignore them? Sometimes we cannot! We work beside them! We carpool together! God urges us to "Go Ye" (Matthews 28;19)! And so, we, are forced to listen to their vulgarity; their loud boasting; their unchristian blasphemy, what then?

Many Christians take every means to stay away from these situations! Hoping someone else will solve these problems. But these are the same type of godless people whom Jesus and His disciples encountered daily! And very likely, they were in the mob who shouted to Pontius Pilate, "Give us Barabbas! Crucify Jesus" (Luke 23:18-21)!

They were affirming: "We know Barabbas —we like his lifestyle. He drinks with us, gambles with us, curses with us —he is our kind of guy— give us Barabbas! Crucify Jesus! Later, as He was being sacrificed, (murdered by this same kind of humanity) Jesus prayed for them (for us) all. "—Farther forgive them; for they know not what they do" (Luke 23:34).

Christ had taught, compassion! "Love your neighbor as yourself." (Mark 12:31) and He has left this "Divine Word," (the Bible) so that we would never forget!

So beloved, when you pray for the (Lost) the one who's lifestyle says, "Give me Barabbas! Crucify Jesus." (Luke 23: 18-21) Call his name out before

Christ as you do when you pray for your own child. Because surely, he, knows not what he does. And because, Jesus said:

"He that is without sin among you, let him first cast a stone... John 8:7)!

God Bless You,

Christ has Come

"Joy to the world the Lord is come." (Baptist Hymnal page 65)

"In the beginning God created the heaven and the earth" (Genesis 1:1). "God created man in His own image...male and female...-God blessed them; He said...have dominion over every living thing...it was very good" (Genesis 1:26-31).

God who knows all things, saw that man would, by himself, fail! Therefore, God issued the first gospel promise to sustain men in their mortal journey: called, "The Protoevangelium" (Genesis 3:14-15. After long struggle this promise was fulfilled: "When the fullness of the time was come, God sent forth His Son to redeem mankind...that we might receive the adoption of sons...into our hearts, crying, Abba Father. ...a son, then an heir of God through Christ" (Galatians 4:4-7). The Bible continues: "Ye also trusted, after ye heard the word of truth, ...ye were sealed with the Holy Spirit of promise, which is the earnest of our inheritance of His glory" (Ephesians 1:13-14).

Beloved, this is what we celebrate at Christmas! Christ came incarnate from heaven, bringing us the opportunity to be saved, converted, forgiven, born again! He still offers this greatest of all blessing to whoever will pray and ask Him! Christ will hear your prayer of faith and redeem your eternal soul! Go before Him in prayer right now, and enjoy your happiest, most blessed Christmas! When you pray that prayer, you will surely sing... "Joy to the world the Lord is come."

> "While shepherds watched their flocks by night, all seated on the ground,
> The angel of the Lord came down, and glory shone around,
> To you, in David's town, this day is born, of David's line,
> the Savior who is Christ the Lord; and this shall be the sign,
> all glory be to God on high, and to the earth be peace:

good will henceforth from heaven to men, begin and never cease."[4]

God bless you,

---

[4] Joseph C. Fisher (Cyber Hymnal page 14186), (www.hymnary.org)

Clear Vision

"Where there is no vision, the people perish" (Proverbs 29: 18).

Society is slipping into, secularism! There is a sense of darkness, of helplessness, of unsolvable questions. It suggests our text. There, is moral decadence, civic mistrust, and religious failing among our people: Whether it be: national, state, city, school, business, or church. Our vision is struggling.

There can never be clear vision without fervent prayer and our prayer has been neglected! But prayer remains our greatest weapon: of greater value than any plan, program, or process. If a manufactured solution would fix the world, our problems would have been solved long ago, Prayer alone is our answer! We must learn God's will first, rather than making our plans and then saying, "God Bless"! Every great leader is a person of great prayer!

Moses prayed and passed safely through the Red Sea. Pharaoh scoffed, and his army passed away, in the Red Sea! King, David filled the Psalms with supplications, but his greatest failure was in neglecting prayer as he looked at Bathsheba! King Solomon prayed for wisdom and God made him the wisest in the world. The Apostle Paul learned, "Nothing shall be able to separate us from the love of God" (Roman 8:38-39). Jesus Christ prayed until Gethsemane soaked up the bloody sweat of His fervency! Every great leader has been a man of great prayer!

John Knox prayed, "give me Scotland or I die"! Scotland had National Revival! John Wesley prayed, "for one hundred prayer warriors"! God gave him the United Methodist Denomination! Dwight Eisenhour prayed, "Give me courage to make the decisions, I must and leave the results to you"! George Washington prayed; he rose to win American Independence! Abraham Lincoln prayed for Emancipation! Charles Spurgeon said, "prayer pulls the cord down here, that sets the prayer-bells ringing in heaven!"

"Where there is no vision, the people perish" (Proverbs 29:18). Let us pray for our land and leaders, ourselves and faith, our churches, and their witness for a lost and dying world.

God bless you!

Conformed to, What?

"Brethren...present your bodies...acceptable
unto the God" (Roman 12:1).

We are very interested in our personal impression! We make our best showing because what others think is so important to us. We have an image that we present to the world. When someone criticizes our appearance, we are offended! Example: We ask, "How does my hair look?" The answer: "Your hair looks a mess today!" We are embarrassed, upset because that was not the answer we expected! We react the same about weight, manners, conversation. We are easily injured!

Paul makes us wonder: what does God think? This world is selfish, prideful, conflicted. Conforming to this world means embracing these things, becoming a part of them, exerting the strength of life involved in them, and presenting the sick sated result to God! Beloved, what does God think? God does not create junk; sin does that!

God often sees our mind; reprobate; carnal; blinded; alienated; conformed to this world. Dear friend, God says, "Be not conformed to this world." (Roman12:2) "Whatsoever things are true, whatsoever things are honest, whatsoever things are just, whatsoever things are pure, whatsoever things are lovely, whatsoever things of good report, if there be any virtue, and if there be any praise, think on these things" (Philippians 4:8). What is God's acceptable will.

"Be not conformed to this world: but be ye transformed by the renewing of your mind, that you may prove what is that good, and acceptable, and perfect will of God." (Roman 12:2)

God bless you!

Covenant Prayer

"Now the God of peace, that brought again from the dead our Lord Jesus…through the blood of the everlasting covenant… make you perfect in every good work to do His will…through Jesus Christ" (Hebrews 13: 20-21).

Brother, sister, young person: has the corona virus exhausted you? The length of it? The danger? The financial burden? Are you fatigued? Beloved, you need a purpose, a work that you can do, a task that has a real meaning and will truly bring results in the battle we are fighting! For instance

I knew of a young boy (18 years old); not big, not brave, not a hero on the football team—just a skinny youngster who finished high school and was immediately drafted into the U.S. Navy: He was afraid! We gathered to see him off to boot camp. The last to say farewell was his foster mother. She said "I know you are afraid. I do not know where you will be sent, or what dangers you will face. So, I will make a covenant between myself and you, and Jesus. Whatever you need, at noon each day I will pray for you. Do your duty and do not be afraid."

A year later he was ordered to perform a dangerous mission! Kenneth responded, "Captain can I wait till twelve o'clock?" His superior asked, why! The boy replied: "At noon my mother will be praying for me I won't be afraid!" Brother/sister there are thousands today: hospitalized; alone, and afraid! Others ill at home unsaved, afraid! Still others; quarantined, not knowing their future! Find one of these and make a covenant: you, and them, and Jesus Christ! Every day; at a certain time; that you will be praying their name before God! Beloved you can do this if you will! Make a "covenant prayer" your daily mission! Let us not grow weary in the Lord's work; but call upon our heavenly Father

"…through Jesus Christ…" (Hebrews 13: 20-21)!

God bless you!

Crying Out to God

"Then began men to call upon the name of the Lord"
(Genesis 4:26).

Here is a significant Scripture! This is the early generations of mankind on earth. And it appears there is chaotic communication between man and God. What tragic events this first family endured:

The serpent, sin, and expulsion from the garden! Assigned to a "God–cursed" environment! One son murdered, the other banished! What heartbreak, Adam and Eve suffered because of their sin! Cain was banished to the land of Nod. No word that his people ever followed God! But Adam's third son, Seth, is born and Eve praised God (verse 26). "Then men began to call upon (to pray) the name of the Lord" (Genesis 4:26)!

Latter sin prevailed (chapter 6), and Noah was the only person "...who found Grace... (Genesis 6:8). His family was saved and carried God's gospel into the post–flood world. However, somewhere in their midst, the "sin-seed" was hidden and survived. Noah's grandson, Nimrod, rose to build Babel.

All of this, great tragedy! Little prayer! And we remain much the same today. How often, too often, someone has endured terrible hurt; tried every solution, then confessed, "I've tried everything I know, all I can do now is pray!" And we think, why is praying the last resort? Why not the first? Why is man so reluctant to pray?

And so, man continues few praying, many not! Even so today, saying what good is prayer? Satan has planted his seed very deep! But Jesus has provided forgiveness at the cross for every man. He brought "grace and truth" to earth. Grace, to forgive, truth, that there is answered prayer! Grace to always love you, and truth to always hear you, when "men, (you) began to call upon the name of the Lord" (Genesis 4:26).

Beloved, keep on calling!

God bless you!

Daniel's Prayer Purpose

"Daniel purposed in his heart that he would
not defile himself" (Daniel 1:8).

God has a plan! The sun, moon, and stars are fixed in their orbits where the Creator placed them. The sun rises and sets on schedule, the seasons follow each other in sequence! And God has a plan for humanity. "The steps of a good man are ordered by the Lord" (Psalm 37:23).

Satan introduced sin, physical illness, and physical death into God's perfect creation. Sin is the poison that all mankind must fight throughout life, and it takes all to the grave. But God has redeemed us when we pray and believe in Jesus Christ as Savior. Once "saved," we can return to the plan God has for our life because. "As many as received Him (believed Christ), to them gave He, power to become the sons (and daughters) of God, even to them that believe on His name" (John 1:12).

How shall we live within God's Plan? What did Daniel do?

1. He vowed to live without intentional sin! "But Daniel purposed in his heart that he would not defile himself" (Daniel 1:8). He set a goal!

2. Daniel made plans to achieve his purpose! He said to his captors (Eunuchs): "I beseech thee, ten days...give (vegetables) and water... then see if we are acceptable" (Daniel 12-13). (No fat food or strong drinks for me). A good vow for anyone!

3. Daniel followed his plan! "At the end of ten days, he was fairer... God gave him knowledge, skill, and understanding in all wisdom and dreams" (Daniel 1:15-17).

4. Daniel with God's help and strength, pleased the king! "The king communed with Daniel... and found none like him...and he continued before the king ..." (Daniel 1:18-21).

Beloved: Purpose to pray, find a daily place to pray, follow your plan! Succeed! God will bless you!

Remember: your steps are, "...ordered by the Lord..." (Psalm 37:22).

God bless you!

Directions for Prayer

"My voice shall you hear in the morning, O Lord; in the morning will I direct my prayer unto thee and will look up" (Psalm 5:3).

David, the great "prayer- voice" of Israel, is faithful to make this promise to his Heavenly Father! And in most part, David kept his covenant! A lifetime later, we find his final prayer, "praise ye the Lord" (Psalm 150:6). David was never at a loss for words! I have asked those to pray who responded: "I cannot! I never know what to say! For these here is a partial list of subjects, in which you may approach your heavenly Father, in Jesus's name:

Pray with thanksgiving — "Thanksgiving and honor, be unto our God forever and ever Amen" (Revelation 7:12).

Pray with authority — "Get thee behind me Satan! Thou art an offence unto me" (Matthew 16:23).

Pray with confidence — "When He shall appear, we may have confidence, and not be ashamed" (I John 2:28).

Pray about salvation — "The grace of God that brings salvation, …to all men" (Titus 2:11).

Pray with intercession — "He (Christ) can save them…He ever liveth to make intercession for them" (Hebrews 7:25).

Pray with repentance — "The Lord is not willing that any should perish, but that all should come to repentance" (2 Peter 3:9).

Dear Friend, it is too often that the one who refuses to pray are those who do not read the Bible. The Bible says, "Thy word have I hid in my heart, that I might not sin against thee" (Psalm 119: 11). How shall I know if I have sinned if I do not read the Bible. The Apostle Paul said about himself: "I had not known sin, but by the law" (Roman 7:7. Pray my brother! The

Holy Spirit will convince you to study God's word! His word will teach you, His will; then you will say like King David:

"In the morning will I direct my pray unto thee" (Psalm 5:3).

God bless you!

Dorcas Sat Up

"Peter put them all forth, and kneeled and prayed; and said Tabitha arise, and she opened her eyes: and when she saw Peter she sat up" (Acts 9:40).

Tabitha's name was also called, Dorcas! She became sick and died. She was prepared for burial and laid upstairs. The people sent for Peter. He dismissed the mourners, kneeled beside the dead, and said: "Tabitha, arise and she sat up" (Acts 9:40). "It was known through all Joppa; and many believed in the Lord" (Acts 9:42). Beloved, here is the greatest ministry in the world— prayer! Here is the resurrection power of God in Christ! Jesus did not teach preaching, He taught praying. He was much in prayer, at times all night. The disciples said, "teach us to pray" and He did. (Luke 11:1)

Praying is a ministry in which everyone can participate! All are not called to preach, or sing, or be a missionary but all can pray. It is the greatest of all worshiping! Just think every program, process, conclave, has been tried and our world remains lost! If the intellect, education and planning of man could prevail, it would be done! What must happen? God must change the spiritual heart of people! How? Through the prayers of God's saints! World-wide revival takes world-wide prayer-warriors, are you willing?

This is very possible! The Lord said. "If you will, I will" (II Chronicles 7:14). Spiritual awakening is not new to our Heavenly Father. But it takes a "want-to" from His people! It occurred in 1734, 1800, 1858, and in 1906. The world we know today was spared by prayer and revival.

We have been praying that God will pour out His Holy Spirit once again: in every church house, every schoolhouse, every courthouse, every jail house, and every dwelling house in our conner of the earth. Let it begin here! Too big an undertaking? Not for God!

Let us kneel like Peter! Pray like Peter! And wake the spiritually dead!

God bless you!

Even So, Come, Lord Jesus

"And this gospel of the kingdom shall be preached in all the world for a witness unto all Nations; and then shall the end come" (Matthew 24:14)!

Life becomes so terrible, somewhere in the world, that it causes some to declare "Surly, this is the end of the world!" In times of flood, famine, and unimaginable loss, it is earth's final hour!

Yet we recall Noah and the World-Wide Flood; individual Apostles and Prophets; Two World Wars and worst of all, the crucifixion of our Lord Jesus Christ! Still God's mercy holds; the world still stands! Why? The answer, God is not willing that any should perish; "God so loved the world, that He gave His only begotten Son, that whosoever believes in Him, should not perish but have everlasting life" (John 3: 16).

This transition which marks the end of life must be experienced by every human being! For some death is expected, accepted, and even welcomed. Others view death with great fear, panic, and horror. It comes to some with surprise; even through all know that one day; the Death Angel must arrive at our personal self!

I have been at the bedside of numerous people, heard their final words, as they met the end of life: the unbeliever, the atheist, struggles with life's greatest surprise and panic! Some who could never make up their mind about Jesus. The skeptic finds that Christ has called for them "like a thief in the night" (1 Thessalonians 5:2). Others, pretenders, seem to argue Have we not done thus and so for you Lord?

I have never seen a true, praying Christian, fight against death as they slipped into the presence of God. Some have said, "I see Mama;" "these people are beautiful;" "This is the most wonderful place I've ever seen;" never an expression of fear, hesitation, or regret.

Beloved, pray now about tomorrow that, Land of Perfect Day, and when it is time, let your prayer be, "Even so, come, Lord Jesus" (Revelation 22:20)!

God bless you!

Faith, Prayer and Fasting

The Disciples asked, "Why could not we cast Him (the lunatic boy's demon) out?" Jesus said, "Because of your unbelief-howbeit this kind goeth not out but by prayer and fasting" (Matthew 17: 19-21).

A miracle! amazing, to His followers! Jesus explained the reason they had failed: because of little faith, weak praying, and lack of fasting." Indicating that they, (even we) could find great power in prayer if we would comply. Do we? Are we living close to Jesus Christ? Are we accustomed to praying? Prayer has power. Some of these tell us this is true:

"Lord Jesus cause me to know the glory of thy name and teach me how to use it in my prayer. Thy name secures me access, is my plea, secures me my answer. Blessed name. Honey in my mouth, music in my ear, heaven in my heart, all in all in my being." (C. H. Spurgeon) "Not many people like to pray, yet prayer is the soul's communion with God and the foundation of all our power in the gospel, O Lord how we need to pray!" (W.A. Criswell)

Whatever you shall ask in My name, that will I do, that the Father may be glorified in the Son. If you ask anything in My name, I will do it" (Jesus Christ; John 14: 13-14).

Beloved, Christian, these things concerning prayer are not about magic they are about faith. Your personal faith (belief, trust, confidence) in Jesus Christ, the Son of God, whom you have received as your Savior and Lord. About your prayer life, do you pray? It is about "fasting." Have you given up those things that once came between you and God?

If you are sincere, pray, in Jesus's name and God will forgive all those things (sins). That is what Jesus meant when He said, "Howbeit this kind goeth not out but by prayer and fasting" (Matthew 17:19-21).

God bless you!

Faithful High Priest

"Wherefore in all things it behooved Him (Christ) to be
made like unto His brethren, that He might be a merciful
and faithful high priest in things pertaining to God, to make
reconciliation for the sins of the people" (Hebrews 2:17).

Jesus came (sinless, incarnate) to save His people! They were sinful, with
no means of forgiveness. God accepted the sacrifice of Jesus as payment
for the sins of mankind and saves those who believe in Christ! Jesus came!
The sinless gave His life for the sinful!

Jesus also came to be obedient to God. As He gave up His life He prayed,
"Father forgive them for they know not what they do" (Luke 23:34).
His shed blood was given to fulfill the will of God. It was the will of
God always that His people "grow in grace and in the knowledge of our
Lord and Saviour Jesus Christ" (2 Peter 3:18). Jesus brought "propitiation"
(sacrifice, sanctification, payment, appeasement before God) for sin! Sin
is so terrible that its cost was and is the eternal and spiritual death of man.
"The wages of sin is death" (Roman 6:23). Every person sins, so every
person must die! The son of God came and died for every human and paid
sin's penalty.

But Christ rose again—proving that all who believe in Jesus Christ, who
pray and asks Him for salvation who lives according to His teachings,
will rise to live forever also! It is the most crucial decision you will make
in your lifetime! Pray, ask Jesus for your salvation: Beloved, Don't Miss
Heaven—Christ died for you!

> "Sweet is the promise, I will not forget thee:
> Nothing can molest or turn my soul away.
> Even tho' the night be dark within the valley,
> Just beyond is shining one eternal day." [5]

---

[5] Charles Gabriel 1856-1932 song "I Will Not Forget Thee" (www.hymnary.org)

"He that believes on the Son (Jesus Christ) has everlasting life: and he that believes not the Son (Jesus Christ) shall not see life; but the wrath of God abides on him" (John 3:36).

God bless you!

Father's Guidance

"Pure religion and undefiled before God and the Father are this, to visit the fatherless and widows in their affliction" (James 1: 27).

"In the beginning," man, "Adam" was given life first. But he was not complete; why not? The Bible explains: God said, "it is not good that the man should be alone" (Genesis 2:18).

God made a woman (Eve) and brought her unto him! "Therefore, shall a man leave (his family), cleave unto his wife and they shall be one flesh" (Genesis 2: 22-24). All "others" are man's arrangements!

God gave man purpose: –"God put him into the garden to dress it and to keep it" (Genesis 2:15). Also, Adam, was to have dominion over "every living thing that moved upon the earth" (Genesis 1:28).

The father who loves and provides for his family; both physically and spiritually is indispensable! Being one who lost my father at an early age, I know the value of the father's hand! More than once I have stood, fearful and uncertain, needing my father's direction!

Yet at eight years of age, my father led me to Jesus, my heavenly Father, who has kept me throughout life: This was the greatest thing he ever did! If you have such an earthly father, make sure on Father's Day you thank God for him!

The saddest thing we face today is the absence of the godly fathers, both in the home and in the church!

God bless you!

From Childhood to Adult

"When I was a child I spake as a child…" (1 Corinthians 13:11)

We human beings are, "Fearfully and wonderfully made marvelous are thy works; and that my soul knows right well" (Psalm 139:14). My Lord, you have created me with the capacity to know and judge even myself: "For if we would judge ourselves, we should not be judged" (1 Corinthians 11:31). And it is within me to do this; it is called "introspection"! We can do this if we will.

The Bible tells us: "So God created man in His own image, in the image of God created He him; male and female created He them" (Genesis 1:27). And this includes the ability to consciously step outside ourselves and take an honest look at oneself; mentally, physically, spiritually, and emotionally. If we are honest, the Holy Spirit will reveal our spiritual health to us.

This is so important; to my spirit, my soul, my mind, my emotion: because: "As he (she, me, you,) thinks in his heart, so is he" (Proverbs 23:7). "Keep thy heart with all diligence; for out of it, are the issues of life" (Proverbs 4:23). Therefore, as we perform our process of "self-introspection" we can determine, if and where, sin may have entered in. Beloved we know ourselves! We know our lifestyle! We know as we look through the lens of introspection if what we see is pleasing to God or not. Let it be that we do not dismiss a sin as being a harmless habit.

We fail to remember all the sins of our life, (but God remembers) and have never repented of them. King David had the same concern: therefore, he prayed: "Remember not the sins of my youth" (Psalm 25:7). Let us pray and use these supplications to complete our text:

"…I understood as a child, I thought as a child; but when I became a man (women, adult, Christian), I put away childish things" (1 Corinthians 13:11).

God bless you!

From Danger into Blessing

"And He (Christ) withdrew Himself into the
wilderness and prayed" (Luke 5:16).

What has just occurred? What prompted Jesus to hurry away from the very people to whom He had come to save? It was because of His growing fame! Jesus had just healed a man of Leprosy. He charged the person to "tell no man" (Luke 5:14). But he or someone else did. And the word went out that Jesus was a great healer. The Bible says, "There went out a fame abroad of Him: great multitudes came together to hear and to be healed by Him of their infirmities" (Luke 5:15).

The people were clamoring to see this Jesus, as they thought, work His "magic," and witness the halt and lame recovered. They were most intent upon the physical healing and missing His soul-saving message. This misplaced popularity plagued Jesus many times; John 6:15 relates; "When Jesus saw that they would make Him King, he departed again into a mountain Himself alone," he knew that earthly fame could prove to be a disaster. He was always about His Father's business, and so should we be the same!

We must pray and learn that the "wilderness times" are often for our own benefit. Periods of deep grief; times of hard decisions; may be of God's grace. We should pray and grow spiritually in these wildernesses! Our Father is always teaching His children; even in the difficult hours of life; especially in the prideful times. Beloved, the pride of life can overtake any of us; but Jesus has our answer! Pray! He says, "Come unto me, all ye that labor and are heavy laden (including sorrow, loss, pride, prestige, or fame), and I will give you rest" (Matthew 11:28).

Make your "wilderness" a season of prayer, and Jesus will lead you through it a stronger person. Be assured that every "wilderness" that you enter will increase your faith and grow you into a greater Christian witness when you emerge on the other side. With Jesus Christ guidance, you will be victorious.

God bless you!

Fruitful Prayer

"...all things, whatsoever ye shall ask in prayer..."
(Matthew 21:22)

Bro. Mark learned to like the Pastor, and finally to trust him. He helped around the church from time to time. The church struggled back then, and Bro. Mark felt needed – welcome. He was a native of Mississippi, his wife was from Georgia. Neither of them had much formal education and were suspicious of others.

The Pastor retired and I was called as Pastor in 1986. The congregation consisted of twenty- two members including Bro. Mark wife. He could not give up his liquor, it amounted to one pint of whiskey per day!

Mrs. Mark began a season of daily prayer that God would deliver her husband from his bondage to alcohol. She never relented! She prayed for many months: in fact, she became one of our most faithful "prayer warriors." She was faithful in every way: women's ministry, nursing home ministry, and attended every church service. Always, she kept up her intercession for her husband!

One Sunday God answered! Bro. Mark came forward, gave his heart and life to Jesus Christ, was baptized, and never drank again! What a glorious answer to prayer! What a victory! God promised, and God answered! Bro. Mark said he suddenly lost his desire for the whiskey he had craved for so long! And he knew his wife had prayed the addiction out of him!

There is more! He also smoked! After his "alcohol deliverance," he would slip around, and attempt to hide his smoking habit. We asked him, why? He told us! "I'm afraid my wife will see me: she'll begin praying for me, and God will make me quit that too!"

Both these dear souls are in heaven today. And both are witnesses to the power of God's promise, "And all things whatsoever ye shall ask in prayer, believing ye shall receive" (Matthew 21:22)!

God bless you!

Garbage Dump Rose

"God shall deliver them from the wicked
and save them ..." (Psalm 37:40)

Here is a truth if we trust always in Jesus Christ. Do not allow "evil-doers" to consume your thinking: Pray for them! God can deal with every situation!

Here is the "worry account" of, "The Rose in the Garbage Dump." A man, very dejected was taking his daily exercise. He was so overcome by his dilemma that he took the wrong turn. He passed a large garbage dump. Flies and insects swarmed everywhere and there was a terrible odor.

As he hurried past, the man observed a sight which both astonished him and stopped his progress. Growing from the top of all this filth and rancid garbage was the most beautiful red rose he had ever seen!

The astonished man burst out: "What are you doing in a place like this?" To his amazement the rose answered, "I did not choose this, I asked God the same thing. He said, trust in me, commit thyself to me, do not fret, "wait upon the Lord, those who wait shall inherit the earth" (Isaiah 40:31), so I obey God! I waited! I prayed! and I made some decisions!

I decided to grow as tall as possible so that passers-by would notice that I am different! And to grow as beautiful as possible so that people could see that God grows Grace and beauty out of ugliness!

I decided to smell as lovely as possible so that I may show everyone what God will do even in the worst of environments! And God has not forsaken me, I have found contentment even here. So, can you!

The dejected man went on his way praying, meditating, leaving his fears and terrible worries at the garbage dump!

Recalling the witness who said… "The salvation of the righteous is of the Lord He is their strength…" (Psalm 37:39).

P.S "Don't worry, I know that roses don't talk"

God bless you!

God Chose You

"Create in me a clean heart, oh God; and renew
a right spirit within me" (Psalm 51:10).

One of the greatest conflicts between our relationship with God is when we give up on his promises! We pray! He has promised to answer! But the answer is not forthcoming, and the most frustrating thing is for us to wait! If we are a seasoned Christian, we know that God is not trifling with us so, what is going on?

The Lord answers prayer, always, in our best interest! Faith tells us He has delayed for our benefit. Never think that God is tempting you. "For God cannot be tempted with evil, neither tempts He any man" (James 1:13). Christ will never be cruel simply to see us suffer, but He will "test" us! Why? Perhaps to strengthen us for what is ahead!

Perhaps to remind us that "Every good gift comes down from the Father of Lights, with whom is no variableness, neither shadow of turning" (James 1:17)! Or the Father has chosen to "Keep you in perfect peace, whose mind is stayed on Thee, because He trusts in thee" (Isaiah 26:3)! God has a special word for you, or some unique labor to complete, or a lesson, that we must learn!

God picks whom He will and equips them for His service! No one was more unwilling or less prepared than Jonah to bring Faith to Nineveh, but with God's power he succeeded (Jonah chapter 1-3). And who would choose William T Seymour to ignite the famous "Azusa Street Revival" in Los Angeles, California?

God did! And then came Mordechai Hamm, preaching and praying thru North Carolina. Seeking whomever God would save! Here the Lord chose an unlikely farm boy named, William Franklin Graham, Jr. and molded him into "the most influential Christian leader" of the 20th century.

Beloved if you are willing, God will choose and use you, "and then will (you) teach transgressors (God's) ways; and sinners shall be converted Unto Thee" (Psalm 51:13).

God bless you!

God My Helper

"My help comes from the Lord, which made
heaven and earth." (Psalm 121:2]

The Psalmist testifies to this eternal truth when he declares: "I will lift up mine eyes unto the hills, from which comes my help" (Psalms 121:1). Beloved where else would we turn? The song of J.B. Coats confirms, "striving alone to face temptations sore, where could I go but to the Lord?"[6] And then Jeremiah, settles this matter in God's word: "Before I formed you in the belly, I knew thee and before you came forth out of the womb, I sanctified thee and I ordained thee" (Jeremiah 1:5). Then the Bible instructs us explicitly, "Let us therefore come boldly unto the throne of grace, that we may obtain mercy, and find grace in time of need" (Hebrews 4:16).

And so, we look up and pray to God our Father, in Jesus' name, in times like these! We have permission; we have instruction; we have expectation of success, and we must pray. Many are in trouble. For some this has been a very hard year of sickness, even death! Churches are struggling for people and funds. Job loss has touched others—how do we cope with these things?

We stand on our faith, and we pray! God has not forgotten His people and we must not forget God! These may be tough times, but we are tough people! We must remain faithful in prayer, in church attendance, in our Christian testimony remember, anyone can quit it takes no courage, no integrity, no effort to quit. Think about the Apostle Paul after all his hardships; now facing death; alone in a filthy Roman dungeon. Yet he said: "I have fought a good fight...I have kept the faith" (2 Timothy 4:7).

Pray: for yourself, your family, and the lost; never forget, "My help comes from the Lord, which made heaven and earth" (Psalm 121:2).

God bless you!

---

[6] (J. B. Coats 1940, Banner Hymns 1957 p. 245)

God's Promise to Believers!

"With long life will I satisfy him (the Christian)
and show him My salvation." (Psalm 91:16)

"He that dwell (believers in Jesus) in the secret of the most High shall abide under the shadow of the Almighty. I will say of the Lord, He is my refuge and my fortress: my God; in Him will I trust. Surely, He shall deliver thee from the snare of the fowler, and from the noisome pestilence. He shall cover thee with His feathers, and under His wings shall thou trust: His truth shall be thy shield and buckler. Thou shall not be afraid for the terror by night; nor the arrow that flieth by day; nor the pestilence that walks in darkness; nor for the destruction that wasteth, at noonday" (Psalm 91:1-6).

God gives these sure promises to the believers, to hold to and to keep us from faltering and fearing the impossible times in which we live. God is still in control of your life, your nation, and your future! Trust Him! These are testing times, praying times, and proving grounds! And God will not fail!

Success, safety, honor, long- life and heaven is God's promise to those who believe and prayerfully trust Him. "He shall give His angels charge over thee…because He has set His Love upon me, therefore will I deliver Him: I will set him on high, because he has known my name. He shall call upon Me, and I will answer him: I will be with him in trouble; I will deliver and honour him. With long-life will I satisfy him and shew him my salvation" (Psalm 91:11-16).

Throughout all time God has never changed nor has he failed: he will not now! "I will therefore that men pray everywhere, lifting up holy hands, without wrath and doubting" (1 Timothy 2:8).

God bless you!

God's Hidden Word

"Thy word, have I hid in my heart, that I might
not sin against Thee" (Psalm 119:11).

What a statement! What a promise! What a comfort! God's word: hidden within our spiritual heart, so deeply that death itself can only increase our faith. The Lord's word is magnificent! It is also infallible, inerrant, unchanging, and sublime. To obey Him results in a successfully lived life! It represents a soul that is eternally saved by faith in His Son, Jesus Christ, and one guided by the Holy Spirit each day. Then we have the written voice of God, in human language: So that all people may know the will of God. Within its pages he tells us how we may reach Him at any time, through prayer. "I will never leave nor forsaken thee" (Hebrews 13:5).

Jesus said, "Pray without ceasing" (1Thessalonians 5:17). He modeled prayer: "After this manner therefore pray ye…" (Matthew 6:9) He told us when to pray, "Evening, and morning, and at noon, will I pray…" (Psalm 55:17). Finally, God gives us permission and indicates the place we may pray: "…come boldly unto the throne of grace, that we may obtain mercy, and find grace to help in time of need" (Hebrews 4:16).

The Lord Jesus Himself, prayed long and often about His people and events that concern us. Surely, He intends that prayer is a daily part of our lives: not to be neglected. Christ prayed the whole night thru before he chose His Apostles: He ordained twelve to heal and cast out devils Peter, James, John, Andrew, Philip, Bartholomew, Matthew, Thomas, James, Thaddaeus, Simon, and Judas Iscariot, which also betrayed Him" (Mark 3: 14-19). Jesus prayed in unspeakable agony as He was being crucified: "Father forgive them, for they know not what they do" (Luke 23:34). And Jesus prayed, The Great Commission Prayer, that is still sending missionaries around the world. "Go ye therefore, and teach all nations, baptizing them in the name of the Father, and the Son, and of the Holy Ghost: teaching them to observe all things whatsoever I have commanded you: and lo, I am with you always, even unto the end of the world" (Matthew 28:19-20).

Christian; failing to pray is a sin!

God bless you!

God's Power Over Sin

"All have sinned and come short of the glory of God" (Roman 3:23).

"Wherefore, as by one man sin entered into the world, and death by sin; and so, death passed upon all men, for that all have sinned" (Roman 5:12).

Sin is mankind's greatest problem! And sin is your greatest problem, whoever you are! Sin has separated you from God; the worst disaster that can ever happen to you in your life! But God has made a way back to Himself. The way is faith in Jesus Christ, the only begotten Son of God! "When the fullness of time was come, God sent forth His Son, made of a women, made under the law, that we might receive the adoption of sons, and because you are sons, God has sent forth the Spirit (Holy Spirit) of His Son into your heart, crying Abba, Father, wherefore you are no more a servant, but a son; and if son, then an heir of God through Christ" (Galatians 4:4-7). All this is accomplished through prayer! By salvation! By believing Jesus, God's Son!

"As many as received Him (believed) He gave power to become the sons of God, to them that believed on His name" (John 1:12). Beloved, we must pray and confess to become saved. Our salvation is imparted by God's grace, but we must tell Him our faith (belief) by prayer.

One day Jesus stated the greatness of prayer as they descended the Mountain of transfiguration. The disciples had attempted to heal a demon possessed boy and failed. The boy's father brought the youth to Jesus and Jesus succeeded. His disciples questioned Jesus: "Why couldn't we heal him" they asked, Jesus's answer was, "Because of your unbelief; however, this kind goes not out but by prayer and fasting" (Matthew 17:19-21). Jesus seems to say, there are those things that take a special strength in prayer, and a special lifestyle behind the prayer for there to be success, a life consecrated to God, every moment of each day. May we strive for such a life!

God bless you!

Gossip

"Those things which proceed out of the mouth come from
the heart and they defile the man" (Matthew 15:18)

Jesus is teaching a great lesson, He continues: "Not that which goes into the mouth defiles a man, but that which comes out of the mouth, this defiles a man —out of the heart proceed evil thoughts, murders, adulteries, fornications, thefts, false witness, blasphemies: these are the things that defile a man" (Matthew 15: 17-20).

The Bible teaches that sin begins with a thought: "For as he/she thinks in his heart, so is he" (Proverbs 23:7). Recall the sin of King David: He lingered on his balcony too long, staring at Bathsheba! This resulted in adultery, deceit, lies, drunkenness, murder, and this sin reached into the lives of several others, but it all began with David's thoughts.

We are not what we think we are but what we think, in our heart determines what we are! And the devil continually pours corruption into our spiritual heart. Remember the children's song: "Be careful little eyes what you see, little ears what you hear." That also is apropos for adults! The Bible says: "Let your moderation (forbearance) be known unto men, the Lord is at hand" (Philippians 4:5). God is listening. Further, God's word says: "Finally, brethren, whatsoever things are true, honest, just, pure, lovely, of good report, any virtue, any praise, think on these things, and the God of peace shall be with you" (Philippians 4:8-9).

Gossip and false witness are a part of this sinful way of thinking! What to do? Beloved, we must pray, confess, and ask forgiveness in Jesus's name. Then make some changes in our "thought" patterns! We must develop wholesome, godly intellect! We must let God, through our Lord Jesus, control our thoughts! The Lord says: "He that overcomes shall inherit all things, and I will be his God, and he shall be my son" (Revelation 21:7).

God bless you!

Grace after Grace

"Thou hast dealt well with thy servant, O Lord...for I have believed thy commandments" (Psalm 119:65-66).

Truly here is the testimony of this writer—"It is good for me that I have been afflicted: that I might learn thy statutes" (Psalm 119:71). Your Holy Spirit has been my guide, teacher, and comforter for these many years; and the events of life that I once questioned have turned out to be "for my good," time after time! The events of my life that have resulted in failure have been those when I followed my own leaning: the successes have come when I have prayed first, and then, followed the Lord's direction.

And this is not for me only, but for everyone who seeks God's salvation through "grace and faith" (Ephesians 2:8) and obeys with constant prayer. Charles Gabriel had it right in his great hymn; "From sinking sand He lifted me, with tender hand He lifted me, from shades of night to plains of light, O praise His name, He lifted me." King David shared this same testimony. "The steps of a good man are ordered by the Lord: and he delights in His ways. Though he falls, he shall not be utterly cast down: for the Lord holds him with His hand. I have been young, and now am old; yet have I not seen the righteous forsaken, nor his seed begging bread" (Psalm 37:23-25).

Then Jesus teaches us a powerful lesson... "Forgive us our debts, as we forgive our debtors...for if we forgive men their trespasses, your Heavenly Father will also forgive you: but if you forgive not...neither will your Father forgive your trespasses." (Matthew 6:12-15)

Beloved, let obedient prayer guide your life and you will surely say: "You have dealt well (successfully)

with your servant, O Lord..." (Psalm 119:65).

God bless you!

Grandma Faith

"If you can believe, all things are possible to
him that believes" (Mark 9: 23).

Believe simply means you have faith? We are challenged with this question in the Bible or lack of it! Remember Paul's account of Demas and his failed faith. Demas had been numbered among the "fellow laborer's" of Paul when prayer was requested. "But withal prepare me also lodging for I trust that through your prayers, I shall be given unto you. Salute Epaphras my fellow prisoner in Christ Jesus; Marcus, Aristarchus, Demas, Lucas, my fellow laborer's" (Philemon verse 22-24).

Later Paul wrote to Timothy, "Do thy diligence to come shortly unto me: for Demas hath forsaken me, having loved this present world ..." (2 Timothy 4:9-10). That is where Paul's message had convicted Demas ... now he is weary with well doing and has deserted! His faith may be called "Demas-Faith"!

My grandmother was a teenager in the backwoods of East Texas just before the First World War. Life was very hard! They lived by faith, which is mostly all they had! But she also had a testimony about God she shared with me! A drought occurred! It failed to rain, week after week, the cotton died, the cornstalks wilted; water wells dried up; the forest turned brown! What to do? Finally, they decided to pray for rain. There were two churches in their county, a Baptist, and a Methodist! Grandma attended the Baptist!

The people came! They overfilled both churches! And they prayed! Grandma said she had never heard such weeping and praying! All over the woods! And it rained! And the people shouted! God filled the ditches, creeks, and the Sabine River flooded out of its banks.

Grandma lived to be old! A hard life! She never left the woods! And she never wavered from her faith in God! She had watched the horses and mules drink from the wagon ruts that day!

I call that "Grandma-faith"! How is your faith holding up?

God bless you!

Greater Grace

"… the sons of God came to present themselves before the Lord, and Satan came also among them" (Job 1:6-10).

Satan's Method:

Satan wants to possess your soul! What are his methods? He promises us what we want! Our weak nature is quickly overcome. We see, touch, or feel the desire of our lust, and we return for more. World War 1 (popular song): "How you goanna' keep 'Em down on the farm, after they've seen Paree?"

One of our greatest temptations is television, internet, cell phone, iPod, etc.; because they are available, and provide pornography. So often, (1) The person takes a look, (2) the look (temptation) looks, (3) and the look takes the person!

Satan's Myth:
This sin only affects lost people.
Church people are not affected to become users.
People can stop using pornography any time they chose.

Sin Brings Death:
We are lured away by our own desires.
We yield to sinful desires, and act upon them.
Sin leads to death! Perhaps not physical, but to spiritual numbness. A state where the sin (addiction) does not satisfy, but it must be repeated, more often. We are now in a cycle that is slow death, but we cannot stop. We must have God's help, His Grace, mercy, and strength. Sins may be several: one will be worse ("besetting sin").

The Answer: The answer is God.
Admit your sin. Claim it, it is not God's (James 1:13).
Draw near to God. Name your addition (James 4:8).

Do not repeat your "besetting sin." When Satan returns pray for strength and God's Grace (James 4:6).

Remember, victory is a process, not an event! Freedom may not be easy. No matter how great your sin; the Grace of God is greater, always! He will help you, and you will succeed! "... the offence might abound (be overpowering to you), but where sin abounded, grace did much more abounds" (Roman 5:20).

God bless you!

Having Done All, Stand

"Wherefore take unto you the whole armour of God
that ye may be able to withstand the evil day, and
having done all, to stand" (Ephesians 6:13).

Who? The Christian! Why? To withstand trouble and sin! The Christian is always at war. Against What? Temptation, pride, Satan, and sins of this world. Once the devil gets you started, he begins to "condition" you, that is, you become accustomed to your sin. Then Satan addicts you: it becomes such a part of your lifestyle that you cannot (will not) go extremely far without indulging. It now becomes, "sin that dwelleth in me" (Roman 7:17). Better named, "besetting sin."

It may not seem like a wrong at all. If you think about it, you may disregard it as just a habit. Yet, stop and consider, have you developed such a habit? Has your temper with others grown shorter, your church attendance lessened? Are you neglecting to pray at times? To busy or to pressed. Who is leading you these days? Jesus Christ, or that "man of sin"? Where are your thoughts? "Keep thy heart with all diligence, for out of it are the issues of life" (Provides 4:23). Truly, we all know ourselves. That is why we are created, "in the image of God" (Genesis 1:27). So, we can make choices; decisions; choose right from wrong, and if wrong, we can change.

We can ask God (pray) in Jesus's name to forgive us. He will. He will not only forgive, but He will also send His spirit (the Holy Spirit) to strengthen and lead us. The spirit guides us: physically, spiritually, mentally, and emotionally as we encounter each event of life.

Now there are things we must learn and obey. The Bible says: "Stand not in an evil thing" (Ecclesiastes 8:3). "If we are willing and obedient, we shall eat (enjoy) the good of the land" (Isaiah 1:19). "…Fear not, for I have redeemed thee…thou art Mine." (Isaiah 43:1) "… Having done all stand" (Ephesians 6:13).

God bless you!

Here Am I Send Me

"Also, I heard the voice of the Lord saying, whom shall I send and who will go for us? Then said I, here am I send *me*" (Isaiah 6:8).

Beloved Christians, and sinners alike have been given a second chance? Our gracious Savior has heard our combined prayers; He has lifted His hand of judgement from our world and has extended to us mercy! He has honored our petitions and given relief from the corona virus! His permissive will has allowed illness to descend upon the entire health of mankind because we have turned from His will. Now there shall be healing.

The Bible records previous times when God has used such measures to abruptly gain His people's attention-but with this promise, always "If my people, which are called by my name shall humble themselves, and pray, and seek My face (His will). And turn from their wicked ways; them will I hear from heaven, and I will forgive their sin and heal their land" (2 Chronicles 7:14). Our Lord has allowed our world to undergo decimation for a time, but now given reprieve so that lost men may find Him through salvation, and every Christian through repentance and faithfulness.

And our Father will help us obey! He tells the churches to, "Go and Tell"! The Bible declares: "But ye shall receive power after that the Holy Ghost is come upon you: and ye shall be witnesses unto Me both in Jerusalem and in all Judaea and in Samaria and unto the uttermost parts of the earth" (Acts 1:8). Isaiah asks the question that hampers every church today "—Lord how long?" And God indicates "until the cities be wasted…houses without man… the land utterly desolate" (Isaiah 6:11-12).

God is calling Christian people to work! To be faithful! To pray! Yet we shall not fail! God has spoken victory- "there shall be a tenth… when they cast their leaves (faith): the Holy Seed shall be the substance thereof"

(Isaiah 6:13. Therefore, when Jesus calls to you, my brother; "…whom shall I send," let your answer be

"…here am I send me" (Isaiah 6:8)

God bless *you!*

Holy Ghost Power

"You shall receive power, after that the Holy
Ghost is come upon you — "(Acts 1: 8)

Matthew's account of the resurrection of Jesus records, "Fear not ye: for I know that ye seek Jesus, which was crucified. He is not here: for He is risen as He said. Come see the place where the Lord lay. And go quickly and tell His disciples that He is risen from the dead" (Matthew 28: 5-7).

Mark's Gospel discloses this, "And when they looked, they saw that the stone was rolled away: for it was very great. And entering the sepulcher, they saw a young man sitting on the right side, clothed in a long white garment; and they were affrighted! And he said unto them, be not affrighted: You seek Jesus of Nazareth, which was crucified; He is risen; He is not here: Behold the place where they laid Him. But go your way tell His disciples and Peter that He goes before you into Galilee." (Mark 16: 4-7)

Luke the evangelist recorded: "They entered in; and found not the body of the Lord Jesus. Two men stood by them in shinning garments. … they said unto them, why seek ye the living among the dead? He is not here but is risen." (Luke 24: 3-6)

John gives the account of Mary Magdalene seeing the risen Jesus at His tomb, with instruction to tell His brethren. The same day Jesus appeared to all the disciples except, Thomas. Then, eight days later Christ appeared again to include Thomas.

Jesus appeared the third time by the sea of Galilee. Here, some disciples had gone to fish and the Lord used the occasion to forgive Peter for his denial during Jesus' former trial.

The Holy Spirit came at Pentecost and empowered the Christians to grow the church worldwide to where it stands today. And today,

"For whosoever shall call upon the name of the Lord shall be saved," (Roman 10: 13).

God bless you!

Holy Spirit Prayer

"Praying always with all prayer and supplication
in the spirit…" (Ephesians 6:18)

When we are in deepest need, we pray our best! It is at this point in the Christian life that we learn to supplicate! To touch the hem of His garment. It is at this time of humility, of almost hopelessness that Jesus intercedes, and God answers. I bear this testimony of God's Grace!

In October 1986, my wife and I were called to Pastor, a church in Texas. The church had experienced several splits: and fallen on hard times. The few members left were considering an offer from a local company to sell out.

We began to visit our neighborhood. Some people allowed us into their home, but many did not! We discovered the church had a lot of past controversies! We visited steadily with little or no results. The first year we were ready to quit! Then, as I walked the church yard one day, I learned what it meant to pray with "supplication" and Christ spoke plainly in response, I will bless you!

Beginning that Saturday, we went to the church, knelt at the prayer altar, and poured out our hearts to the Lord. Visitors began to come! Salvations began to happen! And a steady growth took place! We prayed at that altar each Saturday for many years and the membership grew from twelve); to almost one hundred coming on a regular basis.

That is what we prayed for people! The halt, the lame, the down and out, the up and out and especially the lost! God blessed His church because of prayer. We continued our "Saturday night prayer time" for years.

Beloved, if you want your church to grow, God will honor your prayers. Humble yourself and "Praying... watching thereunto with all perseverance and supplication for all saints" (Ephesians 6:18).

God bless you!

Humility

"Humble yourselves in the sight of the Lord..." (James 4:10)

"Humility!" How may we best express it before our Father; before Jesus God's son and our Savior; before the Holy Spirit of God who guides us throughout life? Especially in prayer, by standing, by bowing, by kneeling, and by prostrating ourselves. Let us consider those, great and small, who have been in God's presence.

> King David's Humility- "Then went King David in, and sat before the Lord, and said, who am I, 0 Lord God. ...that Thou hast brought me hitherto? (2 Samuel 718). (For God had said) ... thine house and kingdom shall be established...thy throne forever" (2 Samuel 7:16 18).

> King Solomon's Humility- "In Gibeon, God said, ask what I shall give thee. (Solomon requested) "An understanding heart-between good and evil...to judge-thy great people" (1Kings 3:5;9).

> The Roman Centurion's Humility- "Lord I am not worthy that thou should come under my roof: Speak the word only and my servant shall be healed" (Matthew 8:8).

> The Syrophoenician Women Humility-"She said, truth, Lord: yet the dogs eat the crumbs which fall from their master's table" (Matthew 15:27).

These few samplings show us that it is not what our posture is before God, but how absolutely correct the truth of our spiritual heart must be! God sees the inner man, the soul, the intent, the truth, the true nature of what we are! God is not mistaken. "If I say, surely the darkness shall cover me; even the night shall be light about me. Yea, the darkness hideth not from

Thee; but the night shineth as the day; the darkness and the light are both alike to Thee" (Psalm 139: 11-12).

We must live, speak, think true lives: Say what we mean, and mean what we say! "For the Law was given by Moses, but grace and truth came by Jesus Christ" (John 1:17). Read the Bible, there is the truth you need. Believe the words of Jesus: there is the grace and an abundant life you need! Pray every day, you will be given the grace you require to "Humble yourself in the sight of the Lord" (James 4:10).

God bless you!

I Bow My Knee

"For this cause, I bow my knees unto the Father of
our Lord Jesus Christ." (Ephesians 3:14)

Our prayers should have an intent, a specific, a reason! Surely, we have permission "To come boldly unto the throne of Grace–to obtain mercy… in time of need" (Hebrews 4:16). Yet we must give thought and reverence to the content of our prayers. We need to remain positive, uplifting, and wise in the things we pray about. We must trust in our Lord to work out our impossibilities He has promised to do so. "And we know that all things work together for good to them that love God, to them who are the called according to His purpose" (Roman 8:28).

We may not understand the direction our life is experiencing, and our Heavenly Father is aware of this. He does not hold us accountable for what we cannot yet fathom. But we are to blame if we do not have enough faith to trust Him, and His watch-care over us, and believe beyond the shadow of doubt, that He knows best and that we are in His hands. What did Isaiah say? "Behold, God is my salvation; I will trust, and not be afraid: for the Lord Jehovah is my strength and my song: He also is become my salvation" (lsaiah12:2).

God has a determinate will and a permissive will: Sometimes called His "second-chance will", or His "teaching-will", by which He allows us to make foolish decisions and suffer the consequences to prove to ourselves that God's way is always the correct way. So, let us follow Paul's prayer-pattern in Ephesians chapter three. Strength for God's spirit (v.19); faith (v.17); love (v.17); understanding (v.18); love of God (v.19) and according to His will (v.20-21).

Let this be our "Prayer-Guide" even in the calamity of this corona virus! "I bow my knees unto the Father of

our Lord Jesus Christ" (Ephesians 3:14).

God bless you!

I Saw the Lord

"...I saw the Lord... high and lifted up..." (Isaiah 6:1).

Prayer changes anyone! We are the "perpetuators" of sin; the Bible says, "...all have sinned..." (Roman 3:23) Therefore we must stop our excuses and live righteous lives! Then, we realize we cannot do this by ourselves. We are too weak to overcome temptations. We are slaves to what we call habits. Yet God holds us accountable if they are against His will.

What are these "habits"? Perhaps "liberties" that we take because of thoughtlessness; or our foolish heart which will not listen to God's words read Genesis 4:4-8. In Luke's gospel, the younger brother's demand: "...father give me..." (Luke 15:12), was the sin that later placed him in the pigpen of sin's result. Also, Cain's refusal to honor God's direction led him to murder his brother. We may consider these as blunders that any person might do but they were thoughtless, sinful, selfish outbursts! Outside the will of God! Self-serving!

In 758 BC. King Uzzah died. Confusion was rampant. People were worshiping idols more than God. And Isaiah appears at the temple! He comes to pray and obey the law of Moses; instead, he has a tremendous vision of God! He testifies, "...I saw the Lord sitting upon a throne, high and lifted up, and His train (robe) filled the temple" (Isaiah 6:1). He saw seraphim's (angles)... heard them crying... "Holy, Holy, Holy... the whole earth is full of His glory. "And the posts of the doors moved... and the house was filled with smoke" (Isaiah 6:2-4).

Then Isiah saw himself and confessed, "...Woe is me...for I am a man of unclean lips! And I dwell in the midst of a people of unclean lips...!"! An angel touched him, and God proclaim, "...your iniquity is taken away, thy sin purged." Then the Lord spoke: "...Whom shall I send...?" And Isaiah answered: "...Here am I, send me." (Isaiah 6:5-8) Here is the power of prayer, the grace of God, to change people, and save nations.

Beloved, pray that America will see God as Isaiah did ...High and Lifted up!" (Isaiah 6:1)

God bless you!

I Will Never Leave Thee

"O thou that hearest prayer, unto thee shall all flesh come"
(Psalms 65:2).

Prayer will calm your mind, your heart and soul, especially if you are doing the praying. Are you facing some great temptation? Something you have desired for a long time. And now circumstance has brought this "thing" within your grasp! Yet, to satisfy your desire would be a sin. You know this but you are tempted so strongly that you find no rest!

What to do? My friend pray! Recall God's commandment "O thou that hearest prayer, unto thee shall all flesh come" (Psalms 65:2). Recall the words of Jesus Christ, "God created the heaven and the earth" (Genesis 1:1), who said, "...I will never leave thee nor, forsake thee." (Hebrews 13:5); who promised, "Come unto Me, ...I will give you rest." (Matthew 11:28) Would He now desert you? No! He will satisfy you with His mercy, "...that we may rejoice and be glad ... (Psalms 90:14).

Therefore, God found it necessary to not only change our spiritual heart, soul, and mind at the moment of salvation; but to also fill us with the Holy Spirit. When life has confused us until we do not know what to do, the Holy Spirit will direct us to the correct decision. This occurred at the birth of America. The Continental Congress met to write the Declaration of Independence. There were: many ideas; much confusion, no progress!

Benjamin Franklin said: "I have lived, sir, a long time, and the longer I live, the more convincing proof I see of this truth...that God governs in the affairs of men. And if a sparrow cannot fall without His notice, is it probable that an empire can rise without His aid? Let us pray." They prayed and all articles were finished! America began![7]

When your mind is cluttered, confused, unsure, pray! God will answer you, "…unto thee shall flesh shall come" (Psalms 65:2).

God bless you!

---

[7] Benjamin Franklin 1776 (Https//www.americanrethoic.com)

In God's Care

"Come unto Me..." (Matthew 11:28)

Have you prayed today? Have you placed your work, your family, and yourself, in God's care? Have you visited your prayer room? If not, please do! It is a perfect "prayer closet." A perfect opportunity to touch lives with others!

Isolation is a dangerous path to choose! We only need to look at the leaders of our nation to realize this fact. Both sides stuck behind their own ideas-cannot budge! Cannot change! Certainly, cannot compromise! Consequently, cannot accomplish!

But there is an answer from Jesus Christ! He can tell the way when mankind is confounded! How do we know? Because He has promised the answer and tells us exactly how we may uncover it.

"Come unto Me, all ye that labor and are heavy laden, and I will give you rest. Take my yoke upon you and learn of Me; I am meek and lowly of heart: And you shall find rest unto your soul. For my yoke is easy and my burden is light" (Matthew 11: 28-30).

Perhaps you do not know what a yoke is? A yoke is made to fit over the necks of two horses, mules, or oxen, standing side by side; so that they will work together. The experienced horse is placed at the left front wheel of the wagon. The lesser trained horse stands beside him on his right. They are now a "team." The fully trained one is called "The Wheel Horse." When he is directed left or right, he will turn, and the other horse will follow. Soon they will become a working team together!

Jesus is saying, if we will "Come unto Him..." (Matthew 11: 28) He will "yoke" us to His will and way. We will not be harmed, but helped, because He has an easy yoke (salvation).

We will soon become worker's together, wonderful prayer partners, "...and ye shall find rest unto your souls" (Matthew 11:29).

Beloved, Pray for American; Jesus Christ is the answer!

God bless you!

Infallible Faith

"...Without faith it is impossible to please Him..." (Hebrews 11:6)

What is faith? It is a doctrine! It is a teaching we accept as truth, that we have heard, read, prayed over, and are convinced, it is God's fact! There are numerous doctrines: "the second coming of Christ;" "the virgin birth" many others! All these doctrines fit into our belief system to form our "Christian theology." Today Faith is our doctrine!

The Bible explains: "...faith is the substance (assurance) of things hoped for, the evidence (proving) of things not seen" (Hebrews 11:1). Faith is necessary it is the means of our salvation: "For by grace are you saved, through faith..." (Ephesians 2:8). We must pray always that our faith never weakens, as the man prayed to Jesus, "...Lord I believe; help thou mine unbelief" (Mark 9:24). There may be times when our faith falters, but Scripture tell us, "We are troubled...perplexed...persecuted, but not forsaken...that the life of Jesus might be made manifest in our body" (2 Corinthians 4:8-10). We must remember this, especially now, during the invasion of, corona virus.

Noah was a man of faith. God told him, "I will destroy them (mankind) with the earth" (Genesis 6:13). God said, "make thee an ark..." (Genesis 6:14). Noah had absolute faith in God; he built the ark and mankind was saved. Joshua was another who believed God's word. He was instructed how to destroy the walled city of Jericho. "They marched around the walls; the army; the priests bearing the ark and seven trumpets. The priests blew their trumpets; shouted; and the walls fell" (Joshua, chapter 6).

Beloved, should our faith in Jesus be less than Noah, or Joshua? Should there be the shadow of doubt that He is able to recuse our world from today's pandemic? Let our testimony and prayer be clear, Jesus came! Jesus died! Jesus arose! Jesus Saves! Remember:

"...without faith (absolute, believing) it is impossible to please Him" (Hebrews 11:6).

God bless you!

Intercessory Prayer

"Evening and morning, and at noon, I will pray... "(Psalm 55:17)

Influence in prayer! A Scottish minister prayed that someone would be saved in "todays" service! Someone was — Robert Moffat, who became a missionary to South Africa. David Livingstone heard Moffat preach and became a missionary to Africa! Mackay read Moffat's life story and went to Uganda! Your prayers matter!

How far does your influence reach? Praying for International Missions reaches around the world.

What about closer home? Others you may know more personally. They have sorrows, crises, struggles, these are your mission field also! They include family, neighbors, friends who need God and your prayers.

Those with a child addicted to drugs, a pending divorce, a critical surgery, should drive us to our knees beseeching our Father for mercy on their behalf, this, also, is our mission field!

Rev. R. A. Torrey, once said: "Talking to men for God is a great thing but talking to God for men is greater still."

John Hyde was called, "Praying Hyde"! A mighty intercessor, he was asked, "How can we enlist intercessors for America? He replied, "The only way to get other people to pray is to do it yourself!" Hyde was a missionary to India and a great prayer warrior. It is believed that over 100,000 were saved in the "Punjab Revival" because of his intercession for them!

Your influence will be heard! Intercession will always find the throne room of Heaven! As Charles Spurgeon declared, "When we pull the cord down here, it rings the prayer bell in Heaven and our Father hears and responds."

Remember, those whom God has "Divinely Called" have the same problems you and I have with one added challenge! They are usually placed in an area away from home! Different culture, customs, language, ethnic groups.

We cannot reach them personally, but Jesus can!

So, pray for them, "...and cry aloud and He (Christ) shall hear my (our) voice" (Psalm 55:17)!

God bless you!

Jesus Christ, Praying

Jesus prayed: "Neither pray I for these alone, but for them also which shall believe on me through their word" (John 17:20).

Here is truly the Lord's prayer! We recognize the prayer in, Matthew 6:9-13, as being the form of God's will for us, and so it should be but in John chapter seventeen, Jesus pours out His heart in a divine manner that especially touches the Christian! We urge you, Christian men, and women, to read the chapter yourself right now! Because we believe we are in a world-wide struggle for the souls of mankind! Jesus Christ is the only one able to turn us back to God and every believer is called upon to rise- up in prayer, our power with God!

Beloved, think about what the Bible says! "As for me, God forbid that I should sin against the Lord in ceasing to pray for you... only fear the Lord and serve Him with all your heart ... but if ye shall still do wickedly you shall be consumed both you and your King (country)" (1 Samuel 12:23-25). How often should you pray? "Evening, and morning, and at noon, will I pray and cry aloud: and He shall hear my voice. He has delivered my soul in peace from the battle that was against me: for there were many with me" (Psalm 55: 17-18).

Pray for yourself! Jesus said, "But I have prayed for you that your faith fail not... " (Luke 22: 32) And if you have neglected prayer, trust the Holy Spirit! "The spirit also helps our infirmities: for we know not what we should pray for as we ought: but the Spirit makes intercession for us with groanings which cannot be uttered" (Roman 8:26).

Finally, pray for America for; "What is true, honest, just, pure, lovely, of good report, virtue, praiseworthy..." (Philippians 4:8)

God has promised to "...Hear, forgive, and heal our land" (2 Chronicles 7:14)

God bless you!

Jesus' Mandate

"The spirit of the Lord is upon me... to preach the
acceptable year of the Lord." (Luke 4: 18-19)

Jesus is specific about what this means! He declares: "The Spirit of the Lord is upon Me, because he hath anointed me to preach the gospel (the good news of the Lord) to the poor; he hath sent me to heal the brokenhearted. What else? "Deliverance to the captives recovering of sight to the blind and liberty to them that are bruised." And finally,"...to preach the acceptable year of the Lord!" (Luke 4: 18-19)

Jesus' mandate was: (1.) Preach, (2.) Heal, (3.) Deliver, (4.) Recover, (5.) Liberate, (6.) By Grace through Faith. He sacrificed Himself for the believer's sin, and provided for millions, reaching forward? The Bible tells us: "For all have sinned and come short of the Glory of God" (Roman 3: 23), even the born-again Christians! King David cried out; "Against Thee, Thee only have I sinned..." (Psalm 51:4) The prodigal son wept: "...Father I have sinned against heaven, and in thy sight, and am no more worthy to be called thy son" (Luke 15:21).

The answer is prayer! The Bible says: "Through your sins be as scarlet, they shall be as white as snow: through they be red like crimson, they shall be as wool" (Isaiah 1:18). Again, prayer! "...if any man sin, we have an advocate with the Father, Jesus Christ the righteous: and He is the propitiation for our sins: and not for our sins only, but also for the sins of the whole world" (I John 2:1-2). Pray with faith! Jesus said: "...All manner of sin and blasphemy shall be forgiven unto men... (Matthew 12: 31).

God bless you!

Jimmy Brown

"In as much as you have done it unto one of the least of these my brethren, you have done it unto me" (Matthew 25:40).

How do you treat the "forgotten"? What do you say when you encounter one who is dirty, perhaps ragged, a social outcast? I am reminded of a song about such a boy, the story follows ...

"I sell the morning paper, Sir,
My name is Jimmy Brown, everybody knows
That I am the news boy of the town."[8]

There is a story behind this sad song. One very cold morning, Jimmy passed a church. It was open and warm! He slipped inside and was alone in the sanctuary. He went to the altar and knelt. Not knowing how to pray, he repeated the words: "Jesus, this is Jimmy," over and over.

The Pastor heard the sound and went to investigate. Seeing the ragged and dirty little boy he scolded him. "This is no place for your kind! You must leave!" Frightened, Jimmy ran out the front door! Blinded by his tears, he ran off the sidewalk and into the traffic. He was run over and taken to a hospital. The Pastor followed.

After surgery, a doctor reported that Jimmy was dying. The Pastor went into Jimmy's room to pray for him. Jimmy was whispering, barely audible: "Jesus this is Jimmy, Jesus this is Jimmy"! A glow filled the room! As Jimmy died, the Pastor heard a voice "Jimmy, this is Jesus! Jimmy, this is Jesus!"

We must be careful we never know when we turn away from someone even the unlovely, we do not know his name may be "Jimmy"!

God bless you!

---

[8] By Bert Reisfield and Jean Villard Geils 1948, https://wwwsongfacts.com

John The Revelator's Vision

"...Blessing, and glory, and wisdom, and thanksgiving..." (Revelation 7:12).

Here, we are within John the Revelator's vision of heaven! We see "...a great multitude which no man could number, of all nations, and kindreds, and people, and tongues, stood before the throne, and before the Lamb, clothed with white robes, and palms in their hands" (Revelation 7:9). They are glorifying God "... sitteth upon the throne, and unto the Lamb" (Revelation 7:10). All the angles...Elders, and four beasts fell before the throne on their faces and worshiped God, saying: "...honor, and power, and might, be unto our God for ever and ever. Amen" (Revelation7:11-12).

This vision has an everlasting purpose, question, and answer for each of us! And one of the elders answered, "...what are all these; ...whence did they come from" (Revelation 7:13)? And the elder answered thou knoweth, (in Texas talk), "you know!" The elder said, "...These are they which came out of great tribulation, and have washed their robes, and have made them white in the blood of the Lamb" (Revelation 7:14).

Our question is: are we among this great crowd of the saved? Is our life, soul, mind, cleaned up and ready to join, "The Great Multitude"? Have we prayed? Have we thanked God for His blessings? As we observe Thanksgiving, let us name our blessings and thank God for each one. But most of all, let us thank Him for Salvation, the greatest blessing of all. Then let us pray every day and keep close to our heavenly Father so that, John's vision will become our personal reality as we join "...the great multitude, which no man can number...clothed with white robes, and palms in their hands" (Revelation 7:9).

God bless you!

Just A Reminder

"I exhort therefore, that first of all supplications, prayers, intercessions, and giving of thanks, be made for all men" (1 Timothy 2:1).

What reminder? To organize an association- wide prayer conference that will pray for individuals who do not know Christ as Savior to accept Him: What reminder, until Christians will renew their fervor for the Lord's Kingdom: A reminder, until Christ will grant the "Great Awakening" we are seeking!

We pray for an anointing of the Holy Spirit that brings peace to our homes and our troubled world. That our parents become burdened to bring their children to church and "raise them up in the nurture and admonition of the Lord" (Ephesians 6:4). That our people return to God by the thousands, and not love the world, neither the things of the world (and choose the Lord's church first as Christ has directed) "...not forsaking the assembling of ourselves together..." (Hebrews 10:25).

When I was a boy, revivals lasted for six weeks! Later, they reduced to two weeks. Still later, the norm became one week. More recently, Sunday thru Wednesday (3 days). Today, hardly at all! We no longer sow "Revival Seeds." "Revival Seeds" are sown by Prayer! Beloved, without prayer, churches struggle, lose visitors, lose members, salvations, baptisms, finances, and many close their doors!

We know that we cannot force anyone to pray! But it is this very desire in the heart of people we are attempting to awaken! And Jesus Christ is the only one who can! We must become convicted that the only way to change society is to change people's hearts! And we have the inerrant promise that Christ will make that change.

"If my people, which are called by my name, shall humble themselves, and pray, and seek my face, and turn from their wicked ways; then will I hear from Heaven, and forgive their sin, and will heal their land." (2 Chronicles 7;14)

God bless you!

Keep On Singing

"Speaking to yourselves in psalms and hymns and spiritual songs, singing and making melody in your heart to the Lord" (Ephesians 5:19).

And the textual thought continues even in the next verse of Holy Scripture: " Giving thanks always for all things unto God and the Father in the name of our Lord Jesus Christ." (Ephesians 5:20) Think for a moment how many prayers, praises, hallelujahs, and thankfulness are encompassed in the medium of music for all of us to sing.

Prayers of surrender: "Have thine own way Lord, have thine own way" Baptist Hymnal, p. 355)

Prayers of Christ's Mercy: "He hideth my soul in the cleft of the rock..." (Baptist Hymnal p. 272)

Prayers of absolute assurance concerning our personal salvation: "I know whom I have believed and am persuaded that He is able to keep that which I've committed unto Him against that day."[9] (Baptist Hymnal p. 275)

On and on, song by song, service after service in churches of all sizes and ethnicities we express our praises to the Lord through our prayers set to music. Some people mistakenly say, "I can't sing at all!" And more foolishly joke about, "the roof falling in," if they were ever heard by anyone." But make no mistake, they sing! When the congregation rises to their feet and honors God with — "Then sings my soul, my Savior God to Thee, how great thou art, how great thou art—." (Hymnary.org) It is then that the one who professes, "not to be able," will lift his heart and soul, in feelings beyond himself, and "pray" to God—How great thou art.

The Lord created us with music in our soul. And when we sing His music, we are praying. So do not worry about how well, or less than well, you sing.

---

[9] Walter Hines Sims, Convention Press, Baptist Hymnal p. 355,272, and 275

Remember, you do not pray (sing) for man, the scripture tells us, "The Lord seeth not as man seeth; for man looks on the outward appearance, but the Lord looks on the heart." (1 Samuel 16:7)

So, brother keep on singing (praying).

God bless you!

Keep The Main Thing, The Main Thing

"…my Grace is sufficient for thee…" (2 Corinthians 12:9).

In prayer there is, strength, fulfillment, and answers! Kneel in prayer about some difficultly; When you arise, you may have the same problem, but strength to face, or bear the burden. We do not always proceed from miracle to miracle, but from strength to strength! If God did not allow us to sometimes "work out our own salvation" (Philippians 2:12), we would remain weaklings. Faith- muscles unused will not develop!

I told my grandmother about a problem in the first church I served! To me, it was critical! I expected her to sympathize with me. I was her favorite! She listened to my difficulty. She looked at me and said: "Son, some things, we have to work out for ourselves!"

That answer was not what I expected! It hurt my feelings badly it was not what I wanted to hear! But it taught me a life-long lesson. I prayed but, neither God nor Grandma made my problem disappear! But, as I prayed, God showed me how to successfully deal with it.

After years of ministry and pastoring through uncounted people-problems, I realize how God guided Grandma's advice! When the Apostle Paul had prayed thrice (3 times) about his thorn in the flesh, God 's answer came: "…my grace is sufficient for thee…" (2 Corinthians 12:9) and it was! Paul never mentioned the thorn, again. Instead, he testified at the end of his ministry: "The Lord stood with me strengthened me that by me the preaching might be fully known …and will preserve me unto His heavenly kingdom!" (2Timothy 4:1-18).

Beloved, prayer is also sufficient for you and me! In the worst of times, pray! During times you *do not* understand, pray! In trials that seem unfair, and are unfair, pray! Prayer is the main thing! If you will "keep on keeping on" and "keep the main thing, the main thing," you will understand what the Lord meant.

"...**My** strength is made perfect in weakness" (2 Corinthians 12:9)

God bless you!

Life More Abundantly

"...I (Jesus) am come that they might have life, and that
they might have it more abundantly" (John 10:10).

Life more abundantly! Today people are searching with all their might for direction. We hear them cry help me

education! Another exclaims, how much is enough; money, houses, land, influence, power, the answer comes roaring back from Television Experts, News Media, How to Books, from all areas... "a little more than you have right now. "Get More!" "Climb Higher!" Other voices call out, "who can we believe?" And today, tycoons answer "someone," "they have a degree in X, Y& Z so, they must know, you can believe these people"!

And so, millions follow Doctor So & So, and spend their life attempting to obtain a great amount of, "something," that "someone," has said is, success. But it turns out to be a "will-of-the-wisp," that has cost them their productive years of life, their health, their marriage, their family relations and left them holding a bag of disappointments!

So, can anyone define success? Webster says: "The desired (sense of) or result of a project."

Note: It may be money, promotion, pleasure, position!

But all of these are short-term and at best, temporal.

Once I witnessed a man die without salvation, terrible, as he tried to fight off death! A failed life! By contrast, the Apostle Paul met the close of life with complete confidence, and his testimony: "...the Lord stood with me ...the Lord shall deliver me unto His heavenly kingdom! To whom be glory forever and ever" (2 Timothy 4:17-18).

My friend, life without Christ is a waste and a failure! Life with Christ is full, complete, and death transitions to eternal life in heaven forever an absolute success! His promise: "...I am come that they might have life, and that they might have it more abundantly" (John 10:10)!

God bless you!

Light up the World

"You are the light of the world…" (Matthew 5:14).

And Jesus continues; "…cannot be hidden." (Matthew 5:14) Beloved: a challenge extended a question proposed! In this year of opportunity, who are we? Standing on faith in Christ? Trusting in His saving grace? Who are we spiritually? Are we people of prayer?

How have we chosen? To be great in the world's eyes, or to be loved by our Lord. Who are we? What a question! One that will be judged and tested all the days of our life. Are we soldiers of the cross, or do we cast aside the truth of God when it conflicts with our desire? The Bible says, if you choose you can, "Let your light so shine before men, that they may see your good works and glorify your Father which is in heaven." (Matthew 5:16) Does this describe your life? Is this the person our family sees; our church friends know; the person God is acquainted with?

This reminds us of the standard of today's world; it causes us to ask ourselves "Who are we?" We know the moral, ethical, political, and business standards of society are moving lower and lower are we joining them? Are we leading our family, "…in the nurture and admonition of the Lord;" (Ephesians 6:4) or is society; the theology of Situational Ethics and Secular Humanism teaching our loved ones how to think?

Let us judge ourselves with Jesus Christ as our example! Let us send a good light to those who see us: an honest view; a Christian beacon; a guiding beam; and a flash of warning to those in danger. We will influence many through our lifetime. Let it be for God and good. Who are we? "Let your light so shine before men that they may see your good works and glorify your Father which is in heaven" (Matthew 5:16).

Do not forget to pray each day!

God bless you!

Living by Faith

"...we walk by faith, not by sight..." (2 Corinthians 5: 7).

Man forgets, he is mortal! Many live without the thought of God. Some are (crises prayers)! Seeking God's help at a family illness or deathbed. But when that is averted, go back to their normal lifestyle! No church, no change, no prayer! It is about worldly success, money, retirement planning.

What has God said? "...eye hath not seen, nor ear heard, neither has entered into the heart of man the things which God has prepared for them that love Him" (I Corinthians 2:9). Beloved we must prepare for that time now! "Call unto Me, and I will answer thee, and show thee great and mighty things, which thou knowest not" (Jeremiah 33:3). How definite his words are for everyone! "For I testify unto every man... if any man should add unto these things God shall add unto him plagues... (and)... if any should take away from the words of the Book...God shall take away his part out of the Book of Life ... (Revelation 22; 18-19).

God gave us hind-sight and forgiveness! Also, perception, for the present! And planning but not one second of assurance for our future! We have no foresight at all, we must live the unknow future by faith alone! Faith in ourselves, or faith in God! To the Godless man God gives grace until he passes by death into eternity! To the Christian, God grants salvation now and eternal life in heaven when physical death occurs!

Also, our Father has established an infallible method of communication between ourselves and God, PRAYER! With the Holy Spirit guiding and Jesus Christ interceding, we can reach God at any time.

Through prayer we find salvation and assurance! We find forgiveness and peace! We find our absolute future: once saved, always saved!

Through prayer "... we walk by faith, not by sight..." (2 Corinthians 5: 7)

God bless you!

Look for the Good

"The sufficient grace of Jesus." (2 Corinthians 12:9)

Living itself has proved that parts of life seem not good! Yet the Bible says, "All things work together for good to them that love God—" (Roman 8:28). I have developed a small "Litany" that helps me:

> "Even the hardest times season me for life's crises.
> Even deep valleys prepare me for highest mountains.
> And surely every heartache causes me to appreciate
> The laughter in my life!
> Prayer makes life better than it is bad; makes life sweeter
> than it is not.
> And when I pray God helps me smile." (B. L. Worsham)

Today, a terrible event in the life of the Apostle Paul: but Jesus made it good! Paul was given a heavy burden, but Jesus gave him, sufficient grace! Paul and Barnabas went into Iconium to preach the gospel, and many believed. "But certain Jews came from Antioch who persuaded the people, and having stoned Paul, drew him out of the city, supposed he had been dead. Paul however arose, went back into the city, and left the next morning for the city of Derbe to preach God's gospel" (Acts 14:19-21).

Paul tells of this experience in his personal testimony (2 Corinthians 12:1-6). He suffered the pain of stoning to the point of death but was given the joy of being "caught up into the third heaven (Paradise) and seeing unspeakable things, which is not lawful for a man to utter" (2 Cor. 12:4).

Explained: "...all things (Paul's terrible stoning), work together for good..." (Roman8:28). (Paul enabled to rise and continue; third heaven revealed to his vision): Testified in (2 Corinthians 12:1-4).

My friend live, for Jesus, trust in Jesus, pray in Jesus' name and know without doubting that He will answer your prayers, and provide your needs. You will be convinced: "…My grace is sufficient for thee: for My strength is made prefect in weakness" (2 Corinthians 12:9).

God bless you!

Loving The Unlovely

"Love your enemies, bless them that curse you, do good to
them that hate you, pray for them which — despitefully
use you and persecute you." (Matthew 5:44).

Here is one of the most difficult commandments our Lord ever gave! But
here it is stated, too plainly to be ignored and too emphatically for some to
obey! This requires something dear within us! Something that may find
conflict with our sense of justice! Yet something that exposes our faith in
Jesus Christ, or our spiritual hypocrisy!

Jesus explains the "why" of this scripture: "That you may be the children of
your Father which is in Heaven..." (Matthew 5: 45). And in the desperate
hour of His crucifixion, Jesus modeled this command: "...Father forgive
them; for they know not what they do..." (Luke 23:34) Beloved, "forgiveness
of our sins," the infinite and ultimate act of Grace for which Christ came!
How is it strange then that He should require "Forgiving Grace" from us,
who are saved by "His Undeserved Grace"?

If "love your enemies, bless them that curse you, do good to them that hate
you..." (Matthew 5:44) are things beyond your spiritual growth, do not
give up! PRAY! Next time you are in a difficult situation!

Then, think on these things:

"Kind hearts are the gardens, Kind thoughts are the roots, Kind words are
the flowers, Kind deeds are the fruits!" (Longfellow)

Think on these things!

"Do all the good you can, by all the means you can, in all the ways you
can, in all the places you can, at all the times you can, to all the people you
can, as long as ever you can." (John Wesley)

Think on these things:

"If you love them which love you? ...if you salute your brethren only..., what do you do more than others...? Be ye therefore perfect, even as your Father which is in Heaven is perfect." (Matthew 5:46-48)

Pray, and think on these things, they work

God bless you!

Man's Responsibility

"The duty of man is to seek God! The glory of man is that He is found! "But if from thence thou shall seek the Lord thy God thou shalt find Him, if thou seek Him with all thy heart and with all thy soul" (Deuteronomy 4:29).

The Bible is replete with instances of Christians being urged to call upon God our Father.

"Ask and it shall be given you, seek and ye shall find; knock and it shall be opened unto you" (Matthew 7:7).

"Watch and pray, that ye enter not into temptation: the spirit indeed is willing, but the flesh is weak" (Matthew 26:41). "Hitherto have ye ask nothing in my name: ask, and ye shall receive, that your joy may be full" (John 16:24).

And we find many times when their prayers are answered: (Hannah) "For this child I prayed: and the Lord hath given me my petition which I asked of Him" (I Samuel 1:27). "He shall call upon Me, and I will answer him: I will be with him in trouble, I will deliver him and honor him" (Psalm 91:15).

"If you abide in Me, and my words abide in you, ye shall ask what ye will, and it shall be done unto you." (John 15:7)

We have commands to "...watch and pray..." (Matthew 26:41), from our Lord, Jesus Christ: who gave Himself for our salvation. (Jesus said) "...that men ought always to pray, and not to faint" (Luke 18:1). "I pray for them: I pray not for the world, but for them which thou hast given Me; for they are Thine" (John 17:9).

"What is it then? I will pray with the Spirit, and I will pray with the understanding also: I will sing with the Spirit, and I will sing with the understanding also" (I Corinthians 14:15).

Beloved, from the beginning, mankind has communicated with God through prayer in Jesus' name, and He calls you today, "...pray without ceasing" (I Thessalonians 5:17).

God bless you!

Memorial Day

"And now shall my head be lifted up above mine enemies round about me: Therefore, will I offer in His tabernacle sacrifices of joy; I will sing, yea I will sing praises unto the Lord" (Psalm 27:6).

Here is the season, the day, the time, the hour, when life-hardened strong men will lay aside their tools of craft, and salute "Old Glory," the flag of the United States of America! Not only pay tribute with hand over heart, but also a personal spasm of emotion will unwittingly touch the soul and a tear will moisten the eye, all unbidden; as "the banner of our freedom" is paraded by: As the band is playing, "The Stars and Stripes Forever!" Surely, God lent His grace to John Phillip Sousa as he wrote that greatest of all marches!

Junior Williams was eighteen years old when he stopped by our house to have prayer and say goodbye. He was on his way to enlist for service in World War II. The last we heard he was listed "MIA": missing in France. His body was never found!

Billy Mars was a champion cowboy from Center, Texas. His unit was left on a south sea island to "hold their position" while others were evacuated. There was no other word about Billy.

Rey was a soldier, a family friend. Word came one day that Rey was killed in the water at one of the landings on "D Day"! Junior, Billy, Rey; we grieve, we remember, we honor today!

Never forget to remember on this "Memorial Day" because of thousands like them; "...shall mine head be lifted up above mine enemies..." (Psalms 27:6).

God bless you!

Mr. Jones' Shoes

"Restore unto me the joy of thy Salvation; ... Then will
I teach transgressors thy ways... (Psalm 51:12-13).

Meet, Mr. Jones, and Mr. Smith. They lived near each other. They caught the same bus, at the same time, at the same bus stop! They sat together each day– going to work and returned home!

Every Sunday was also the same! They caught the same bus, but Mr. Jones carried his Bible on his way to his church, while Mr. Smith carried his golf clubs on his way to the golf course! They keep this schedule for twenty years!

One Monday, Mr. Smith, was absent! On Tuesday, the same, and by Wednesday, Mr. Jones knew something was wrong! They had never visited, but Jones knew where Smith lived; and went to inquire. He was informed that Smith had suffered a heart attack and was dying!

He entered Smiths' sickroom and found him conscious! He approached his bed and said, Oh My Old Friend, I am so sorry to see you so ill. Mr. Smith retorted in anger "don't call me friend!" You are not my friend! I am dying, leaving this life, and I do not know where I am going or what is going to happen to me! We have known each other for years we rode the bus together every day and I watched you go to church every Sunday, and you never mentioned God to me! I do not know God. I do not know how to contact Him! You should have told me! I am so afraid! Don't call me, Your Old Friend!

Beloved, could this happen to you? Is there someone, a friend, family member, or co-worker that you need to talk to about Jesus Christ, and repentance, and salvation? Have you hesitated? Then pray for boldness to witness. But what if they get anger?

That is better than you standing before the Lord one day in Mr. Jones' shoes!

God bless you!

My Closest Friend

"That I may know Him." (Philippians 3:10)

It is not enough to know intellectually about Jesus! To read that he exists! That He was an historical person! We must know Him personally as Savior, as Redeemer, as Lord of our life. We must have such an encounter so that we are persuaded His way is better than our way! So that we intend to allow Jesus Christ to direct us from this day forward. This becomes my obsession and desire.

That I may know Him, and whatever He instructs me in His Word (Bible), I will obey because obeying is never a burden: as I follow this "new life" Christ has imparted to me. I find myself so much better off than before. Now, "...we have the mind of Christ" (1 Corinthians 2:16) I see the world from a new perspective! I have a new hope! I am destined for Heaven. Where "... eye has not seen, nor ear heard, neither have enter into the heart of man, the things which God hath prepared for them that love Him" (1 Corinthians 2:9).

This is marvelous! I am saved! Secured within the infallible plan of God. "For I am persuaded... that, height, depth, nor any other creature, shall be able to separate us from the love of God, which is in Christ Jesus, our Lord." (Roman 8:38)

Here is the gift which was conceived by the divine mind of God! A plan confirmed by His Son, Jesus Christ! A redemption that includes forgiveness and eternal life, which gives to all believers, security: "once saved always saved!"

Paul found absolute confidence in this truth! He confirms it in his final testimony "I have fought a good fight, I have finished my course, I have kept the faith: henceforth there is laid up for me a crown of righteousness, ...the

Lord shall give me" (2 Timothy 4:7-8). Beloved, pray for your faith, and God's grace! In that final time, it will be worth it all "That I (you) may know Him…" (Philippines 3:10).

God bless you!

My Father, My God

"He shall cry unto me, thou art my Father, my God,
and the Rock of my Salvation" (Psalm 89:26).

When we address God, it becomes us to use the best language; that is what the Psalmist is attempting when he calls God: "my Father, my God, and Rock of my Salvation" (Psalm 89:26). The best of us is tongue-tied when we are face to face with His awesome Glory!

Yet it is the Lord's mercy that He sees the inner man when we pray; and consequently, discerns the sincere. It is interesting to see what some, important people, from various walks of life, have spoken in prayer, or concerning prayer!

Former President, Dwight Eisenhower, said: "Prayer gives you courage to make the decisions you must make in a crisis and then the confidence to leave the result to a higher power."

Dr. George Washington Carver described his prayer life this way: "My prayers seem to be more of an attitude than anything else. I indulge in no lip service, but ask the great God silently, daily, and often many times a day, to permit me to speak to Him. I ask Him to give me wisdom, understanding and bodily strength to do His will. I am asking and receiving all the time."

John Newton quite naturally expressed prayer poetically: "Then let us earnest be, and never faint in prayer; He loves our importunity and makes our cause His care."

My father, and my mother were singers. Often, they sang: "If I have wounded any soul today, If I have caused someone to go astray; If I have walked in mine own willful way, dear Lord, forgive."

Beloved, how do you pray? out loud? If not, why not? Some respond, "I don't know what to say" which is usually from lack of practice! Exercise your spirit if you love the Lord speak to Him in prayer it is the only way you can!

God bless you!

My Heart is Fixed

"Thy word, have I hid in my heart, that I might
not sin against Thee" (Psalm 119:11).

What a statement! What a promise! What a comfort! God's word: hidden within our spiritual heart, so deeply that death itself can only increase our faith. The Lord's word is magnificent! It is also infallible, inerrant, unchanging, and sublime. To obey Him results in a successfully lived life! It represents a soul that is eternally saved by faith in His Son, Jesus Christ— and one guided by the Holy Spirit each day. Then we have the written voice of God— in human language: So that all people may know the will of God. Within its pages he tells us how we may reach Him at any time, through prayer. "...I will never leave nor forsaken thee." (Hebrews 13:5)

Jesus said, "Pray without ceasing." (1 Thessalonians 5:17) He modeled prayer: "After this manner pray ye..." (Matthew 6:9). He told us when to pray, "Evening, and morning, and at noon, will I pray..." (Psalm 55:17). Finally, God gives us permission and indicates the place we may pray: "Come boldly unto the throne of grace, that we may obtain mercy, and find grace to help in time of need" (Hebrews 4:16).

The Lord Jesus Himself, prayed often about His people. Surely, He intends that prayer is a daily part of our lives: not to be neglected. Christ prayed the whole night thru before he chose His Apostles: He ordained twelve to heal, and cast out devils, even Judas Iscariot, which also betrayed Him, Mark 3: 14-19. Jesus prayed in unspeakable agony as He was being crucified: "Father forgive them, for they know not what they do..." (Luke 23:34). And Jesus prayed, The Great Commission Prayer that is still sending missionaries around the world. "Go ye therefore, and teach all nations, baptizing them in the name of the Father, and the Son, and of the Holy Ghost: teaching them to observe all things whatsoever I have commanded you: and lo, I am with you always, even unto the end of the world" (Matthew 28:19-20).

Christian; failing to pray is a sin!

God bless you!

National Day of Prayer

"Let the words of my mouth, and the mediation
of my heart..." (Psalm 19:14)

"National Day of Prayer"! Every Christian should be praying! Perhaps we could have a stick-on or insignia or a button attached to our clothing, saying, "I am praying"! The Roman Catholics display a cross of ashes on their face showing they have prayed on "Good Friday." Protestants should do the same.

Psalm 19:7-9, spells out several ways we will be changed by prayer and following the mandates of our Lord converting the soul, and causing a rejoicing heart, and God's judgement are true and righteous.

"Prayer" enlightens the eyes of our soul! It enhances perfection! Leads us to purity and is worth more than gold!

Someone said, "I forgot what day it was"! God never forgets the day His Son Jesus Christ was crucified, three days in the tomb, nor the Glorious Resurrection. We must not forget our own salvation! Lord, remind me: "let me be acceptable in thy sight, O Lord, my strength, and my Redeemer" (Psalm19)

> *If I have wounded any soul today,*
> *If I have causes someone to go astray,*
> *If I have walked in my own sinful way,*
> *Dear Lord Forgive.*[10]

God bless you!

---

[10] Arthur C. Battersby, An Evening Prayer, Public Domain (www.hymnary.org)

O God Strengthen Me

"He Sampson called on the Lord…" (Judges 15:18).

Here is Sampson! Physically stronger than any man! A judge of Israel, especially called by God and blessed with the Holy Spirit! But a man of unchecked passions. Sampson was interested only in himself! He called on the Lord only twice. Once, after he had been delivered, as a prisoner, to the Philistines. When they reached, Lehi, his enemies shouted at him. God empowered him, and he broke his fetters. Then with the jawbone of a donkey, "…He slew a thousand men…" (Judges 15:16).

Afterwards he was exhausted, and he prayed: "…Thou (God) has given this great deliverance unto the hands of thy servant; and now shall I die for thirst …"? (Judges 15:18) God answered with a miracle, providing water. The Bible says, "And he (Sampson) judged Israel in the days of the Philistines twenty years" (Judges 15:20).

Yet Sampson continued to follow his own lust. He went to Gaza, a Philistine city. He went into a prostitute. He was surrounded, but he escaped: and "He took the doors of the gates of the city…and carried them to the top of a hill that is before Hebron" (Judges 16:3).

Later he loved a Philistine woman, Delilah! She questioned him until he told her the secret to his strength, "If I be shaven, then my strength will go from me …" (Judges 16:17). Delilah had him shaved! "…the Philistines took him and put out his eyes and brought him to Gaza, bound him with fetters of brass and he did grind in the prison" (Judges 16:21). At a Philistine holiday, they brought blind Sampson out to make sport of him. He pushed down the posts of the building killing thousands, including himself.

His final prayer: "O Lord God remember me, I pray thee, strengthen me that I may be avenged... of my two eyes!" (Judges 16:28).

Sampson, blessed by God, ignored God, his was a prayerless, wasted life!

God bless you!

Omnipotent God of All

"The Lord is my strength and song, and he is become my salvation: He is my God, and I will prepare Him a habitation; my Father God, and I will exalt Him." (Exodus 15:2

From the beginning and throughout all the Bible. It is the theme and thesis of the inspired Holly Book that God is All in All! He is Creator, Father, Son, and Holy Spirit the Almighty, three in one, who is to be reverenced above every thought of man or breath of all living.

It is He who chose His people, Israel, and blessed them with the oracles of God. And who sent, who indeed came, in the person of Jesus Christ, (Emanuel) to die as a human man on the cross of Golgotha, as the only sacrifice for the sins of humanity: Not only that but to rise from the dead and declare: "…because I live you shall live also" (John14:19). those who believe in Jesus Christ as Lord!

Someone has said, Socrates taught for forty years, Plato for fifty, Aristotle for forty and Jesus for only three; yet those three years infinitely transcended the influence of the combined one hundred and thirty years of teaching of Socrates, Plato, and Aristotle. Jesus painted no pictures; yet the art of Raphael, Michelangelo, and Leonardo DaVinci received inspiration from Him. Jesus wrote no poetry; but Dante, Milton, and the world's greatest Poets were inspired by Him. Jesus wrote no music; still Hayden, Handel, Beethoven, Bach, and Mendelssohn reached their greatest melody in His praise. Every sphere of human greatness is because of Christ! But His unique contribution is the salvation of man's soul.

Philosophy could not accomplish this nor art nor literature nor music. Only Jesus can break the power of sin: he can give righteousness to the lost man and enteral life unto the dead. Remember these things when you pray; and proclaim,

"He is my God… and I will exalt Him" (Exodus 15:2).

God bless you!

Original Sin

"Original sin!" "She took of the fruit thereof, and did eat, and gave also unto her husband with her, and he did eat" (Genesis 3:6)!

We read the story (account) of the fall of mankind because of disobeying God. They ate of the "Tree of Knowledge of Good and Evil!" (Genesis 3:6) This introduced "sin and death" into humans!

God created all things: Included in the garden of Eden (Paradise) was also (1) "The tree of life" and (2) "The tree of knowledge of good and evil." (Genesis 2:9)

God gave Adam explicit commandments concerning his future (Genesis 2: 15-17). But "the serpent" (Satan) came and tempted Eve, and she tempted Adam, both ate of the tree of Knowledge, disobeying God! We see their sin in (Genesis 3: 1-7).

Why did Adam and Eve Sin?

1. They were not strong enough to overcome Satan's temptation.

2. We do not know how long they were tempted. Unrelenting temptation overcame them.

3. The tempting finally seemed good to them: Eve first saw that the tree was good for food, pleasant to the eyes, "desirable to make one wise" (Genesis 3:6). Note: These are the exact same temptations that leads us to sin today see (1John 2:15-16). 4. She had influence over Adam, and he also ate. Sin came; death followed (Romans 5:12)!

5. Their spiritual DNA is passed on to all humanity (Romans 3:23).

But God has Intervened!

"For God so loved the world that He gave His only Begotten Son, that whosoever believed in Him, should not perish, but have everlasting Life" (John 3:16)

We all have this choice: "He /she that believes in the Son (Jesus) has everlasting life: and he that believes not the Son shall not see life, but the wrath of God abides on him!" (John 3:36)

Beloved, pray and choose Jesus, Life, and Heaven!

God bless you!

Our Confidence is Prayer

"To Seth was born a son, (Enos): then began men to
call upon the name of The Lord." (Genesis 4:26)

God spoke, first with man face-to- face: "God blessed them and said unto them; Be fruitful and multiply; replenish the earth and subdue it—" (Genesis 1:28) But Adam sinned and broke the covenant between mankind and God! "Who shall deliver me from the body of this death? I thank God through Jesus Christ our Lord…" (Roman 7:24-25) Jesus came: Jesus died; Jesus rose; Jesus saves! Man's solution: grace, faith, salvation, God's gift (Ephesians 2:8)

We have been saved from condemnation to everlasting life by God's grace; thru our individual faith in His Son, our Lord, and Savior Jesus Christ— "For by grace are you saved through faith; and that not of yourselves: it is the gift of God: not of works lest any man should boast." (Ephesians 2:8-9) Salvation comes to us by personal faith and prayer! "—As many as received Him, to them gave He power to become the sons of God, even to them who believe on His name." (John 1:12) To receive salvation, we are to pray and confess our faith: "…Thou art the Christ, the son of the living God." (Matthew 16:16)

Jesus instructs us, "If you abide in Me and My words abide in you, you shall ask what you will, and it shall be done unto you." (John 15:7) God requires a righteous life! He warns us how our prayers may fail:

Sin separates "If I regard iniquity in my heart the Lord will not hear me" (Psalm 66:18).

Self-indulgence "Ye ask and receive not because ye ask amiss, that you may consume it upon your lusts" (James 4:3).

Our confidence in prayer is, "If we ask anything according to His will, He hears us:" (If He hears), "…whatever we ask, we know that we have the petitions that we desired of Him." (1 John 5:15) "…The effectual fervent prayer of a righteous man availeth much" (James 5:16).

God bless you!

Overcomers

"For whatsoever is born of God overcomes the world…" (1 John 5:4).

What then is "the world"? The visible and invisible power of sin! That which tends toward iniquity! The purpose of Satan! These daily influences we must constantly overcome!

Deer brother/sister in Jesus Christ, remember our new nature: Born again! We are a new creature in Christ: "For in Christ Jesus…a new creature" (Galatians 6:15). And having received the Holy Spirit, we cannot sin successfully: The spirit will constantly remind and convict us until we pray and repent. Our text continues and tells us this is so: "And this is the victory that overcomes the world, even our faith." (1 John 5:4)

Now we obey our new and higher master—God is our father; Jesus Christ is our Lord; the Holy Spirit is our guide; and daily prayer is our channel of communication. We realize the Bible is the exact truth of God's word and reading it, we hear distinctly His infallible will and purpose for our personal life. We also find that the ways of the world do not have authority over us–God does! We are convinced that Jesus paid for our sins on Calvary's Cross and guaranteed our resurrection and eternal life at the empty tomb. Read the Scripture—

"What? know you not that your body is the temple of the Holy Ghost which is in you, which you have of God, and you are not your own? For you are bought with a price: Therefore, glorify God in your body, and in your spirit, which are God's" (1Corinthians 6:19-20).

Charles Spurgeon quotes from J.H. Newman: "The gospel of John speaks of the prayerless world as a false prophet. Promising what it can never fulfill: calling it the spirit of Antichrist. By which men are led captive. The answer to the tempter is the spirit of truth, who is greater than he that is in the world."

We must pray daily to gain "...the victory that overcomes the world, even our faith."(1 John 5:4)

God bless you!

Personal Burden

"...I will not let Thee go..." (Genesis 32: 26).

Beloved, do you have a "Burden"? A certain thing that weighed on your heart so strongly you could think of nothing else. The result may cause you joy or despair! Whatever, do you have such a "Burden" today?

Moses had a burden for the sin of his people. He attempted to make atonement himself. He went before God, confessed the sin, and pleaded: "Yet now, if thou wilt forgive their sin –; and if not blot me, I pray Thee, out of Thy book which Thou hast written" (Exodus 32:32). To no avail! Moses did not realize, only the shed blood of God's Son Jesus Christ, can forgive man's sin! Moses' sacrifice was insufficient!

God's answer was, "...Whosoever hath sinned against Me, him will I blot out of My Book" (Exodus 32:33). John Knox, was sincere when he said to the Lord, "Give me Scotland or I die!" And Jacob, holding on to God by faith cried "...I will not let Thee go..." (Genesis 32:26).

> If the world from you with-hold of it silver and its gold,
> And you have to go alone with meager fare,
> Just remember in His word how he feeds the little bird,
> Take your burden to the Lord and leave it there.
> If you trust and never doubt,
> He will surely bring you out.
> Take your burden to the Lord and leave it there.[11]

---

[11] Charles A. Tindley, 1906, Hymnary.org

Perhaps you have such a burden! Your solution is the Lord Jesus. Receive Him as your Savior! If you are a Christian, Keep on praying! Do not stop! Say unto Him, "…I will not let You go, except Thou bless me" (Genesis 32:26).

God bless you!

Personal Sin

"...Be sure your sin will find you out" (Numbers 32:23).

In 853 BC (?), twins were born to Rebekah, wife of Isaac! The Lord explained—Two nations—one shall be stronger—and the elder, (Esau), shall serve the younger, (Jacob) (Genesis 25:23)! Later, Esau, who was called, Edom, (Genesis 25:30), sold his birthright to Jacob (Genesis 25:33); Jacob's name meant, "supplanter" (Genesis 27:36).

Jacob was well named! He deceived his father Isaac and took Esau's birthright; but his irreversible "blessing" also! When Esau threatened his life, Jacob fled to his uncle Laban in Padanaram to escape! There he stayed twenty years tending Laban's herds. But his life of deceit theft continued. Jacob kept the healthy cattle and the weak one he placed in Laban's herd!

Laban became wise, especially as Jacob grew wealthy! Then he slipped away, and his uncle Laban overtook him at Mt. Gilead. (Genesis 31:25) God intervened to bring a covenant of peace between them and Jacob avoided retribution once more! Yet his most terrible day lay before him, saved from his uncle, he must yet face his brother, Esau

Jacob sent messengers! They returned with news, Esau, was coming with four hundred men! "Then Jacob was greatly afraid and distressed" (Genesis 32:6-9). He realized, (Be sure your sin will find you out)! All his wealthy and cunning were no help, and Jacob prayed as he had never prayed! "Oh, God of my Father Abraham..., I am not worthy of least of all the mercies... deliver me, I pray from the hand of my brother... (Genesis 32:9-11). Jacob was left alone, and there wrestled a man with him until the breaking of day" (Genesis 32:24). God's man said, "Let me go...Jacob answered, I will not, except thee bless me" (Genesis 32:26). And Jacob received his blessing! Prayed had prevailed and the blessings were: Jacob's hip was dislocated. His name and status were changed to Israel.

He received grace, forgiveness, and peace with Esau! (Genesis 32 & 33).

Prayer saved Jacob! But consider; how long must a man remain "A Sinful, Jacob," before he learns to become, "A Redeemed Israel"?

God bless you!

Praise From a Stranger

"Let another man praise thee, and not thine own mouth;
a stranger, and not thine own lips!" (Proverbs 27:2)

Beloved, I share a recent testimonial! I conducted a "Memorial Service" for a past member of the church from which I retired, after 32 years. The church provided a meal for the family and friends afterwards.

As we ate, a man approached my table and shook my hand. He said: "When I was a teenager at this church, you took me into your study and counseled and prayed for me. I was developing a drinking habit. I never forgot your prayer! I stopped the alcohol eighteen years ago, and I have had a great life. I just wanted to say, thank you!"

I was able to congratulate him and tell him; "that is the work of God." You see, he had changed so much in eighteen years, I would never have remembered him-but God remembered! And we must never forget: God hears; God answer, God blesses your prayers and now and again, God lets us know so keep praying, God is able!

Remember, the end of each day is, "your sermon for that day. Whatever you have thought, and said, and done or the opposite. what you have refrained from thinking, or voicing, or performing is also what you have preached that day of opportunity!

If anything is bad, go to God, in Jesus' name, and seek forgiveness, strength, and wisdom not to repeat it. If anything is good, thank the Lord for his guidance and mercy. Always give all good credit to God! The Bible says: "for without Me you can do nothing" (John 15:5)!

Practice this lifestyle: refrain from bad; preach what is good; pray about your daily sermon; and life will become a pleasure to live! From time to time "another person may praise you (perhaps God will use, a stranger)."One thing is sure God's will "...His commandments are not grievous." (1 John 5:3)

God bless you!

Pray About Everything

"Pray without ceasing. In everything give thanks: this is the will of God in Christ Jesus concerning you" (1Thessalonians 5 :17-18).

I have heard Christians say: "Do not call on me to pray. I cannot think of what to say." Are you like that? I am constantly researching "prayer," and I ran across the following—it will help those of us who have this problem getting started.

A group of ministers were discussing tough questions that occurred in their counseling sessions. The text "pray without ceasing" came up. One minister was selected to write as essay on the subject to read at the next meeting. A female maid heard their plans and spoke up. She said, "What? Wait an entire month to discuss the easiest verse in the Bible?" "Well Mary, can you pray all the time, especially, when you have so many things to do!" a minister asked?

> *This was Mary's answer! "Why, Sir, the more I have to do, the more I can pray. When I first open my eyes in the morning, I pray, Lord open the eyes of my understanding; While I am dressing, I pray that I may be clothed with the robe of righteousness; When I have bathed, I ask for the washing of regeneration; As I begin my work, I pray that I may have strength equal to my day. I look up to my Father and pray that I may be His child: and so, it is all day. Everything I do furnishes me with a thought for prayer."[12]*

After this little event, the minister's essay on prayer was considered unnecessary. A preacher friend of mine told me: "You could tell the depth of a person's faith and how close his spiritual walk with the Lord was, by how he prayed."

---

[12] *Sermon Illustration, "Elon Foster," Baker Books, 1996)*

Beloved let us labor in prayer often; give thanks to God in Jesus name always; and remember "this is the will of God in Christ Jesus concerning you" (I Thessalonians. 5:18).

God bless you!

Prayer for the Preacher

"… continuing Instant in Prayer" (Roman 12:12)!

Many times, we preach our hearts out, our convictions, our strength, we are exhausted following the sermon, we give the best we have, we extend the altar call, and no one responds, pastors are disappointed!

We have done our best! What more can we give? Perhaps, just perhaps, we have slighted prayer: The most important thing in any service, for example:

Charles Spurgeon, "The Prince of Preachers," was asked; How do you succeed in drawing thousands to your services? He answered, "My people pray for me"! There was a "prayer room" under Spurgeon's pulpit where prayer was offered for his sermon's each time he preached! He, with God's blessings, produced extra ordinary results! Spurgeon called this room "the heating apparatus" of his church!

Dwight Moody preached his opening sermon in London, England, and had no response! He felt it would be useless to preach Sunday evening! A paralyzed lady, whose name we do not know, asked her sister how the service went. The sister said, they had an evangelist from American there, but the people were unresponsive. The bed ridden sister said, "bring me my Bible, I must pray"! All afternoon she prayed for Moody! He, unknowingly, had decided to preach after all. That evening the church was overflowing and the altar was filled, the power of prayer had prevailed!

Billy Graham used this plan while he preached around the world! He always encouraged seasons of prayer preceding and during his crusades. We know the results!

Before our previous associational revival, we had five years of concentrated prayer! It was a success! If you have done your best with little results continue instant in Prayer (Roman 12:12).

God bless you!

Prayer That Shines

"Let Your Light So Shine Before Men…" (Matthew 5:16).

Beloved friend, would you like to cause a major change in your life, beginning now? Find the answer in Matthew 5: 1-16! It comes from the lips of Jesus Christ, and it does not fail.

Christ saw the people, the need, the spiritual hunger! He sat upon a hillside and delivered to them that we may call, "the preamble" of all He had come to teach and fulfill. "The Beatitudes"! Pray over these "Golden Jewels"! Study them closely! Compare them to your own lifestyle! When the Holy Spirit convinces you, make the change!

Approach life with "Humility" (v. 3), "Mourn" for each failure (v. 4), depend upon Faith to keep you "Meek" (v. 5), "Righteousness" will fulfill your soul (v. 6), Christ promises "Mercy-for-Mercy" (v. 7), "Purity" enables spiritual vision (v. 8), "Peacemakers" are offspring of God (v. 9), Suffering for Christ strengthens God's Kingdom (v.10), there are blessings in martyrdom (v. 11), rejoice to share Christ's suffering (v.12) (Matthew 5:3-12).

These things are contrary to the comfortable life, that you may consider to be the good life! Yet when we conform to them, what have we done? With Christ's guidance and strength, we have changed our life! I am a new creature in Christ! I have had a new birth! I now live with humility, repentance, meekness, and righteousness. I am merciful, pure, peaceable, and can deal with persecution! What happened? I have become "…the salt of the earth…" (Matthew 5:13). and each day I am now, "…the light of the world… (Matthew5:14). Some say I could never do this! Yes, you can, a Christian can! Jesus would not require what is impossible! Your answer is prayer, Matthew 5:13-14.

Pray daily with all your heart and you will find God answering, changing you, conforming you and "Let your light so shine before men, that they may see your good works, and glorify your Father, which is in Heaven" (Matthew 5: 16)!

God bless you!

Prayer Wil Overcome

"...God... will not suffer you to be tempted above
that ye are able..." (1Corinthians 10:13).

Temptation is common to every person! God gave man the gift of choice. Satan soon came to the "Garden of Eden" bringing the wrong choice. It is not sinful to be tempted—it is the yielding to sin that corrupts the spiritual soul!

Eve was tempted and chose sin! Adam was presented with temptation; he too sinned. Temptation consumed the earth: "God saw that the wickedness of man was very great, and that every imagination of the thoughts of his heart was only evil continually" (Genesis 6:5). God sent, the flood, destroyed all life, except Noah and his family!

Always temptation is the culprit! If we overcome the temptation, we will not commit the sin! Some may say, God does not love me enough to take a certain desire out of my mind. God says, "...I have loved thee with an everlasting love..." (Jeremiah 31:3). The truth is you have not loved God enough to believe His word! But this sin has haunted me throughout my life, it is not possible to forget! "For with God nothing shall be impossible." (Luke 1:37). Remember!

Moses, trapped at the Red Sea–"Moses said... stand still, and see the salvation of the Lord...and the Lord caused the sea to go back... the Israelites went into the midst of the sea (crossed) on the dry ground..." (Exodus 14:13-22). Our need to overcome today's temptation is no greater than Moses faced, it may seem so to us! I John 2:1, says; "...If any man sin, we have an advocate with the Father, Jesus Christ the righteous: He is the propitiation for our sins..." And never forget.

"…God is faithful, who will never suffer you to be tempted above that you are able; but will with the temptation also make a way to escape, that you may be able to bear it" (I Corinthians 10:13).

Your way of escape is prayer!

God bless you!

Praying for Others

"...Behold, Satan has desired to have you...but I have prayed for thee, that thy faith fail not..." (Luke 22:31-32).

This was the prayer of the Apostle Paul: "Brother, pray for us, that the word of the Lord may have free course, and be glorified, even as it is with you" (2 Thessalonians 3:1). And these are the pleas and wishes of so many of God's faithful, "pray for us!" This is called, "Intercession." Interceding for someone or something apart from our self takes our time, our caring: Someone has called it laboring in prayer. There is power in these sessions.

> *The time is told of Dwight L. Moody's preaching tour in England. Two sisters lived together; one was totally bedridden. However, she read her Bible and spent many hours in prayer. The other sister attended church faithfully. One Sunday the paralyzed one asked the other, "how church went today?" not very well! We had a preacher from America speak. He wasn't very spiritual, and no one came to respond. His name? Moody, I believe.*
>
> *Get me my Bible and close the door. I must pray, which she did, all afternoon, for her church and Mr. Moody. Her sister returned after evening worship, amazed and excited! She said when Rev. Moody gave the invitation, the altar was packed; more in attendance than we've ever had! God had heard and honored her helpless sister's praying. "Intercession!" Moody toured England, revival followed him throughout the entire country of Great Britain! [13]*

In American, there has occurred three wide-spread Awaking's, Renewals, Revivals! Times when God moved in the spiritual hearts of our nation and

---

[13] Dwight L Moody, 1872, Public Domain (Wikipedia.org)

by His grace called us back to Himself. These movement happened after great sessions of prayer.

Can God do it again? Yes! Will He? That depends on us! What we value; how we live if we intercede! Beloved, will you pray for: the lost, the sick, the abused, the youth, marriages, and Christian morality.

"For my love…I give myself unto prayer!" (Psalm 109:4)

God bless you!

Proto-Evangelium

The Incarnation! The Greatest Miracle in the World! The First Christmas! Jesus Christ is born among mankind to save believers from their sin!

He was predicted from the beginning! Adam and Eve sinned, paradise was lost, but God cursed Satan and said: "I will put enmity between thee and the women, and between thy seed and her seed; it shall bruise your head, and thou shall bruise his heel" (Genesis 3:15). "The Proto-Evangelium," (first promise of the gospel).

The prophet Micah, received from God, the place of Messiah's birth! "Bethlehem Ephrathah though thou be little among thousands of Judah he shall come forth unto me that is to be Ruler in Israel; whose goings forth have been from old, from everlasting" (Micah 5:2).

Rome held God's people captive! They prayed for Messiah! And "...he angel Gabriel was sent from God...to a virgin...and the virgin's name was, Mary...the angel said—behold you shall conceive...and bring forth a son... and shall call His name, Jesus" (Luke 1:26-31)!

Jesus still comes to save! We know a lady who prayed for her husband many years! Three weeks ago, we baptized Him! Beloved, Christ does not fail us, we must never fail Him in prayer!

His promise: "...And all thing whatsoever you shall ask in prayer, believing, you shall receive" (Matthew 21:22)!

Have a blessed prayer filled, Christmas, and keep on believing!

God bless you!

Read the Problem

"And the world passes away, and the lust thereof; but he that
doeth the will of God abideth forever" (1 John 2:17).

A trigonometry professor at the University of Texas in Austin told us: If
you do not remember anything else in this course, remember, "RTP" Read
the Problem! More people fail at more things in life because they do not,
"RTP"! I read and re-read: But it still took two semesters before I passed
Trigonometry. I was told that I was "right–brained" and "left- brained" but
at Trigonometry I was "no-brained"! However, I will never forget, "RTP"
and it has stood me in good stead these many years.

Have you purchased an item in a container that said, "easy to assemble"?
It appeared that a child could do it. But when you finished, you have
parts left over and your product works incorrectly, or not at all. What is
wrong? You failed to "RTP"! Many approach life in this same manner!
Just dive into "things" and see what happens: alcohol, drugs, gambling,
sex. pornography, without "Reading the Problems" that may follow!
Whatever life presents, "RTP," the old folks always told me: "Look before
you leap."

Where to look? The Bible! What to recognize? Sin! What to remember?
Salvation! Who to believe? Jesus Christ! I highly recommend that
throughout your life, you will stop and pray., and "RTP." When you
have read, think of the values of the world. Mankind has reached
the place that he calls: Noise, music! Spaced-out superstars, heroes!
Unbridled sex, love! Pornography, art! Homosexuals, alternate lifestyles!
Abortion, people's choice! School prayer, a crime! Success, power! Sin,
fun! Money, God!

And the basic theology of many, who have no doctrine at all is "Universalism," God will save everyone! Christ has said: "...the world passeth away!" (1John 2:17) Beloved, be constant in prayer and in doing God's will! And above all

"Don't Miss Heaven"!

God bless you!

Receiving Your Answer

"Jesus Answered...bring him hitherto me" (Matthew (17:17).

We are attempting to learn all that we can about communicating with our Heavenly Father! So how do you pray? With assurance? Or with doubt? Do you take your burden to the Lord and leave it there; completely, without reservations?

In our text, Jesus' disciples have experienced unanswered prayer! Why? "Bring him to Me. Then, Jesus rebuked the devil: ...and the child was cured. The disciples said," ... why could not we cast him out. And Jesus said unto them, because of your unbelief: ...if you have faith as a grain of mustard seed, you shall say unto this mountain, remove hence, ...and it shall remove; and nothing shall be impossible unto you" (Matthew 17:17-20).

What are we dealing with here? Clearly, the unanswered prayers of the disciples of Jesus! This child's father testified in Matthew 17:16, "I brought him to thy disciples, and they could not cure Him." And Jesus pointed at the missing elements, lack of faith (v. 20) and fasting (v. 21) (Matthew 17: 16-21).

Have you prayed for a person or event that is "too deep for words"? Too personal to speak about. And that prayer remains unanswered! It may be about your own besetting sin! And this one thing continues to defeat you? Beloved, have you obeyed God to the fullest? Is this an answer that, "this kind goeth not out but by prayer and fasting?" (Matthew 17:21) Was this word from Jesus something He simply said in passing or is it the way that we may be worthy to possess the "power of prayer" that we so long for.

Pray about this, my friend! About fasting and not only about food and drink. But about giving God full and complete control of whatever, and whoever, is nearest and dearest to you!

Then, He may give you the power to deal with your answer in return!

God bless you!

Redeeming Grace

"For by Grace are you saved through faith, and that
not of yourselves: it is the gift of God: not of works,
lest any man should boast" (Ephesians 2:8-9).

"For by grace are you saved through faith..." by the undeserved love of God "...not of yourselves...", you cannot save yourselves, "...it is the gift of God", God, sent Jesus to die in your place: and believing in Jesus as your Lord and Savior, you are saved, "...not of works..." not because of any good things you have done, "...lest any man should boast". the sin of pride is within every person; therefore, it is excluded (Ephesians 2:8-9).

Beloved the Bible says, Jesus' speaking: "For God so loved the world, that He gave His only begotten Son, that whosoever believeth in Him should not perish, but have everlasting life" (John 3:16). And this scripture follows: "He that believeth on the Son has everlasting life: and he that believeth not the Son, shall not see life; but the wrath of God abides on him" (John 3:36). God requires that you love His Son, Jesus and love your fellowman, and instructs you in the Bible the daily life you are to live. Remember this:

When you read the Bible, God is speaking to you; when you pray, you are speaking to God! We are commanded: "Pray without ceasing. In everything give thanks: for this is the will of God in Christ Jesus concerning you" (1 Thessalonians 5:17-18). You have great power with God, through Jesus Christ, and He wants to hear from your heart.

"Is any among you afflicted? let him pray! Is any sick among you? let him call for the elders of the church...! And the prayer of faith shall save the sick...sins they shall be forgiven him. ...the effectual fervent prayer of a righteous man availeth much" (James 5: 13-16). And let it be, "...as ye would that men should do to you, do ye also to them likewise" (Luke 6: 31).

God bless you!

Salt and Light

"You are the salt of the earth, and the light of
the world—" (Matthew 5: 13-14).

Jesus does not ask; He tells us who we are (who we are supposed to be!) When we believe in Christ as our Savior and pray for His guidance every day; stand on His grace, trust His promises always, we can become "Salt" and "Light".

We can: "Let our light so shine before men, that they may see your good works and glorify your Father" which is in heaven" (Matthew 5:16). Beloved, who are we? We must take stock of ourselves often. Conduct a spiritual inspection to determine if we are achieving these goals! When we seek the answers with all our heart; the Holy Spirit will direct us correctly! We must continually pray!

"Salt" is a preservative! It keeps flavor fresh; it keeps good things from going bad. "If the salt has lost it savor, …it is good for nothing…" (Matthew 5:13) That is why we pray so often, so that our witness for Christ is always salty (fresh, sincere, effective).

"Light" is to be seen! The light that Jesus gives should shine for everyone to recognize. There should be no such thing as a "secret disciple." Jesus ignited God's love light when He saved us. We are born again, re-born, regenerated, converted, we are a new person in Christ, (2 Corinthians 5:17). Let it be known! You've been given the grace of God and you carry the words of salvation. You are a Christian! Walk like one! Talk like one! Shine like one! Pray like one!

Beloved Christian, who are we in God's eyes? Are we salt that purifies, preserves, flavors? Are we "light" that beckon, guides, invites? Are we witnessing, winning, welcoming? What sermon do we preach each day?

"Let your light so shine before men, that they may see your good works, and glorify your Father which is in Heaven" (Matthew 5:16).

Don't forget to Pray!

God bless you!

Sanctified Prayer

"Sanctify ye a fast, call a solemn assembly, and all the inhabitations of the land... cry unto the Lord" (Joel 1:14).

Joel teaches that God uses disasters to warn His people to repent! "The palmer worm...the locust–the canker worm...and the caterpillar...hath laid my vine waste and barked my fig tree...the day of the Lord is at hand..." (Joel 1: 4-15).

God gives a sever warning: the invading armies (Babylon) from the north are coming!

"Blow the trumpet in Zion...let the priests the ministers of the Lord, weep between the porch and the altar, and let them say, spare thy people, O Lord..." (Joel 2: 15-17).

"The Lord will answer... I will restore you... (and)...I will pour out my spirit upon all flesh; and your sons and your daughters shall prophesy... whosoever shall call on the name of the Lord shall be delivered ..." (Joel 2: 25-32).

Non repentance brought judgement upon God's people! The exile! and years of captivity, yet God did not forsake (Joel 2: 19, 3:1-21). Israel did not dream that God would allow them to be destroyed, but He did! When they repented, God Blessed!

What about American!? Founded on, "In God We Trust!" We sing "God Bless America!" But as a people, what do we do? Our church life, and prayer-life is ignored! The Bible says! "Not forsaking the assembling, ourselves together... as we see the day approaching" (Hebrews 10:25). Our sins are comparable to "Noah's day"! "...the wickedness of man was great... every imagination of the thought of his heart was only evil continually" (Geneses 6: 5).

Our God is money and pleasure! The Bible says, "Neither be ye idolaters; as some of them, as it is written, the people sat down to eat and drink and rose up to play" (I Corinthians 10:7).

Jesus says, "…except ye repent, ye shall all likewise perish" (Luke 13:3).

Jesus says, "As many as I love, I rebuke…(repent)" (Revelation 3:19).

Jesus says, "I come quickly… to give every man according as his work shall be" (Revelation 22:12).

Jesus says, "If my people will… pray, … I will forgive…" (II Chronicles 7:14).

God bless you!

Sin and Death

"The wages of sin is death…" (Romans 6:23)

Max Lucado writes in Unshakable Hope: (Nashville: Thomas Nelson, 2018): "The Bible names a real and present foe of our faith: the devil. The Greek word for Devil is 'diabolos' which means 'to split.' The devil is a divider. He divided Adam and Eve from God and wants to divide us from God."

He uses his power to tempt you, (saved and lost alike): to yield to his obscure suggestions and commit sin against God's will. It may be a small sin at first, something of little consequence. But it has introduced you to a thought, word, or deed: and to a lifestyle that, the Bible says, is death, (Roman 6:23)!

The tendency will be to repeat that "little sin" again! It becomes easier: and it grows! Truth is, you have become weaker! You have become accustomed to yielding to temptation.

I knew a boy from my hometown. He was a good boy. He told me this sordid story, weeping as he related it! He went out with some other boys in our college town. They obtained some alcohol and urged him to join them in drinking, so he drank. They went into a bad part of town, met a girl, paid her for her favors, and indulged, including my friend. I have never forgotten his words to me. He said, "I have prayed all week for forgiveness. I know God has forgiven me, but I have soiled my soul forever."

Beloved, Baran Group shows: four out of ten Christians (40%) agreed that Satan is only a symbol of evil. Only 35% said Satan is real. Most Christians do not believe in his existence. Jesus said he is real, your enemy; temptation is real, and sin is death!

But "… the gift of God is eternal through Jesus Christ our Lord" (Roman 6:23).

God bless you!

Sometime Alienated but Reconciled

"You that were sometime alienated...In your mind... "(Colossians 1:21)

The hidden danger in isolation!

We need encouragement! We need each other! Not isolation! Eve would never have partaken of the "forbidden fruit," if she had not faced temptation, alone! Alone is where we may find ourselves most vulnerable!

Remember, every sin begins with a thought, a fantasy, an unguarded moment, which allows Satan to slip in a vision of temptation! The Bible says, "For all have sinned and come short of the Glory of God" (Romans 3:23); and again, (Roman 5:12) "...all have sinned!"

Achan, heard, Joshua's command, "And ye, in any wise keep yourselves from the accursed thing...gold, silver... (Joshua 6:18-19)! But temptation overcame, Achan, (Joshua 7:21), "I saw... a garment...silver... gold... and took them!" King David, did not plan his acts of adultery, lying, and murder, when he was tempted with Bathsheba, but they all followed isolation and temptation, (2 Samuel, (Ch. 11)!

Do not isolate yourself! Come and pray with us! The opportunity to pray is available to you. Are burdened, stressed with some wrong thought, no matter what, Jesus Christ will strengthen you to declare, "...Get thee behind me Satan..." and when you do, Satan will flee (Mark 8:33).

Prayer is your powerful weapon! Defeating your most powerful enemy, who can destroy you, if you allow! But Satan has a master, the Lord Jesus Christ, whom he must obey. When you call on your Master, Savior, Hope, and King of Kings, "... the devil, and he will flee from you" (James 4: 7) Depend upon Jesus, because "...yet now hath He reconciled" (Colossians 1:21)!

God bless you!

Speaking Salvation

"Arise go to Nineveh, that great city, and cry against it..." (Jonah 1:2).

Do you believe in "second chances"? Do you give "second chances"? God gave Jonah a "second chance"! What does Christ expect from us?

Jonah refused God and ran away! "Jonah. went down to Joppa ... found a ship... and went down... to go to Tarshish from the presence of the Lord" (Jonah 1:3). Notice: each time Jonah ran it took him further downward, away from God!

We are the same! When we know God's will: have heard it from the pulpit, have read it in the Bible and we knowingly, intentionally disobey, we are separating ourselves from His Kingdom! When we obey, we have pleased God, and drawn closer to reflecting Jesus Christ!

Sometimes it is difficult! The sin is so tempting! It is such a little sin. The adage works well for any temptation, "the person takes a drink, the drink takes a drink, and the drink takes the person!" Try repeating this to your heart when you are staring temptation (Satan) in the face.

We must cry with Job: "...make me know my transgression and my sin" (Job 13:23). Let our prayer be: "God forbid. How shall we, that are dead to sin, live any longer therein" (Roman 6;2)? "Knowing this... that henceforth we should not serve sin" (Romans 6:6).

We find, Jonah, did obey God. But how much greater to be the Lord's willing servant. Beloved we must make up our mind up-front! That is to decide now to learn God's will and pledge not to sin against Christ even when Satan presents the opportunity. Jonah's prayer of surrender must become our prayer! "I will sacrifice unto Thee with the voice of thanksgiving; I will pay that, I have vowed, salvation is of the Lord" (Jonah 2:9)!

God bless you!

Springtime has Arrived

"The flowers appear on the earth…" (Song of Solomon 2:12)

Springtime has arrived in our land, let us sing and rejoice! The dark and terrible winter of pain and loss is swiftly receding into its place of darkness, and God has brought a new season of hope-of joy-of salvation! This is the season for small children to frolic; to fill the air with innocent laughter. It is the time that calls teenagers to baseball, football, and cheerleading. School bands are marching; music is in the air. Wedding bells, long silent because of "Covid-19 concerns", ring with extra chimes. Christians are free to greet one another with handshakes in the churches and familiar smiles are exchanged from unmasked faces, a new time has arrived.

We sing together again! We pray together; our testimony says welcome: "For lo the winter is past, the rain is over and gone, the flowers appear on the earth; the time of the singing of birds is come, and the voice of the turtle is heard in the land. The fig tree puts forth her green figs, and the vines with tender grape give a good smell…. —Let me hear thy voice…for sweet is thy voice…" (Song of Solomon 2:11-14).

My friend, God has brought a new year and is blessing His people! Shall we not, in turn, pray and thank Him for His grace! Shall we, read His Bible? Attend His church? Obey His commandments? Speak his name in daily prayer"?

"…The time of singing…is come…" (Song of Solomon 2:12)

God bless you!

Stepping in the Light

"The steps of a good man are ordered by the Lord." (Psalm 37:23)

What keeps the downtrodden singing, Happy am I, PRAYER! What causes the heartbroken to find, Victory in the ashes, PRAYER! What gives Hope to the frightened and moves them to proclaim, "Lord give me that mountain, PRAYER! What motivates the Christian to declare, "Though He slay me, yet will I trust in Him..." (Job 13:15) PRAYER!

What gave unyielding courage to the Great Deacon, Stephen? He who is the "Proto Martyr" (first martyr)! The first Christian who was killed for his faith in Jesus Christ! As Stephen prepared to die, he said "...behold I see the heavens opened and the Son of Man standing on the right hand of God" (Acts 7:56).

Have you wondered why Jesus stood? The Bible says that "Jesus is set down at the right hand of the throne of God" (Hebrews 12:2)! Yet at the execution of Stephen, "Christ Arose"! Have you thought the reason was to give courage and high honor to His Faithful Deacon, who was, "...Full of the Holy Ghost..." (Acts7:55), and proved it with his testimony, and his life!

What an honor, that Christ, the Son of God, the glory of heaven, should rise in readiness to receive His Faithful Servant! And what an effect this event had on, Paul. Paul the Apostle, who consented to Stephen's martyrdom (Acts 7:58 & 8:1) and who some years later said, "I am now ready to be offered... I have fought a good fight... henceforth there is laid up for me a crown of righteousness, which the Lord... shall give me at that day: not to me only, but unto all them also that love His appearance." (2 Timothy 4: 6-8)!

Beloved, is this your testimony? Are you longing for that day? Is your daily wish, "...Even so, come Lord Jesus!" (Revelation 22:20). Let it be, when Satan whispers ("defeat"), you will PRAY and "Wait on the Lord and He Shall exalt thee to inherit the land...(Heaven)" (Psalm 37:34).

God bless you!

Surrendering to Prayer

"...I give myself unto prayer" (Psalm 109: 4).

We have come far in our journey of prayer! Gathering after gathering, broadcast following broadcast, multiple articles to encourage brothers and sisters of the ministry of prayer! It is the greatest single work of God in all of Christianity. Our Heavenly Father ordained prayer as the means of direct communication between man and Himself, in the name of His Son, Jesus Christ. Jesus declares, "...I am the way, the truth, and the life; no man comes unto the Father but by Me" (John14:6). Pray in His name!

God tells us how to pray: "Let us therefore come boldly unto the throne of grace, that we may obtain mercy, and find grace to help in time of need" (Hebrews 4:16). If you are not a Christian, God tells you how to become one: "...everyone which sees the Son (Jesus), and believes on Him, may have everlasting life: and I will raise him up at the last day" (John6:40). Accept Jesus Christ as your Savior!

And if you are a Christian, Christ instructs your life: "For we are His (God's) workmanship, created in Christ Jesus unto good works, which God has before ordained that we should walk in them" (Ephesians 2:10). Obey God's Bible!

God rejects no one who will believe and call on Him for salvation. Rather, it is we who may reject God, and condemn ourselves to eternal condemnation! He tells us, whosoever, may pray! However, the doctrine of prayer is neglected, seldom used as the main topic of sermons. We are rushing to speak "our words," rather than, take time to be guided by the Holy Spirit's direction. "The spirit (Holy Spirit) also helps our infirmities: for we know not what we should pray for as we ought..." (Roman 8:26).

Beloved, there is great comfort; there is assurance; answers; blessings in the ministry of prayer. Rev. Billy Graham was asked: "Billy what more would you have done? Graham's answer: I would have studied more and prayed more!"

God bless you!

Sweeter Than Honey

"The full soul loatheth an honeycomb; but to the hungry
soul every bitter thing is sweet" (Proverbs 27:7).

Have you read this "truism"? Have you pondered its double meaning? Bread and water will relieve the physical problem, but only salvation will solve spiritual starvation. To live the "abundant life" that Christ provided; each soul must have both bread and redemption.

When my Great Grandparents married, they had no money, limited supplies. They planted cotton. A dry summer followed. The crop failed. They ran out of food. An apple tree produced some fruit. They picked apples, and ate fried apples for breakfast, stewed apples for lunch, and baked apples for supper. After several months wild turkeys came thru the woods, and they hunted them for fresh meat.

Grandma was saved shortly after that. Grandpa, a little later. He became a Baptist preacher. I am told they were a wonderful, caring, couple: But Grandpa never really liked apple pie.

The lost man is the same, as our text! He has no hope of God's Glory even when he fills his stomach a thousand times. Alcohol will not satisfy his hungry. Neither will drugs, money, or worldly success. Jesus declared "For what is a man profited, if he shall gain the whole world, and lose his own soul... (Matthew 16:26). Beloved what is the value of your soul?

When you support "Global Hunger" pray this prayer: "The full soul loatheth a honeycomb; but to the hungry soul

every bitter thing is sweet" (Proverbs27:7).

God bless you!

Take Up Your Cross

"He that taketh not his cross, and follows after Me,
is not worthy of Me" (Matthew 10:38).

God assigned Adam to be the caretaker of the world! "And God said, let us make man in our image, after our likeness: and let them have dominion over the fish of the sea, and over the foul of the air, and over the cattle, and over all the earth, and over every creeping thing that creepeth upon the earth" (Genesis1:26).

God forbade only one thing–"But of the tree of knowledge of good and evil, thou shall not eat of it: for in the day that thou eatest thereof thou shall surely die" (Genesis 2:17). "… the woman saw that the tree was good for food and that it was pleasant to the eyes and a tree to be desired to make one wise, she took of the fruit thereof and did eat and gave also to her husband with her and he did eat!" (Genesis 3:6) Paradise was lost! Sin and death entered the human race!

Sin was manifest in the first generation of Adam's offspring: Cain killed Able! Since then, there has been wars, weapons of warfare, men seeking to commit war, and rumors of war among every tribe and nation, always.

Hear the words of Jesus Christ: "You shall hear of wars and rumors of wars…these things must come to pass…nation against nation…famines and pestilence and earthquakes in divers places. False prophets shall rise … the love of many shall wax cold … But he that shall endure until the end, shall be saved" (Matthew 24: 6-13).

And Matthew chapter 24 &25, tell us of the chaos even until the Lord returns, and the final judgment is complete. What can we do? The Bible tells us exactly!

Jesus said, "Come unto me...I will give you rest... learn of me...ye shall find rest unto your souls." (Matthew 11:28-29). Therefore brother/sister, Pray! Make prayer your burden and your cross. Find peace and joy even in confusion and be worthy of our Lord!

God bless you!

Temptation

"Watch and pray, that ye enter not into temptation…" Matthew 26:41)

"Sin" is your enemy: but "temptation" is the pathway to it! Therefore, we must do something

about "temptation"! There is the downward tendency of sinfulness; and the upward tendency of righteousness, which is:

The more we succumb to temptation, (whatever it is), the easier it becomes to sin; the more often temptations (of various kinds) will be presented to us and the weaker our resistance becomes! This is the "downward tendency"! Conversely, the more we refuse temptation, (whatever it is), the harder it is for sin to overcome us, and the less temptation we will encounter and the stronger Christian we become this is the upward tendency of righteousness"!

Jesus knew the subtle danger of "Temptation"! What did He say? "Lead us not into temptation…" (Matthew 6:13). Pray that God would keep us from the "slippery-slop" that leads to sin. Prayer gives us strength to avoid and overcome the tempter! But when we continue to follow Satan's deceiving invitation, we will finally, sin, the sin then we are guilty! And unless we pray for forgiveness, we may well commit the damming thing again, often! Someone has voiced it like this:

Sin- will take you father than you meant to go!
Sin- will keep you longer than you meant to stay!
Sin- will cost you more than you meant to pay!
We think, "It's not so bad; I know of worse"!

After all, you say, a glass of wine, a flippant word about Christ, a boastful lie among friends, really? But sin none the less! And we are in danger! Of weakness, of slipping away from Jesus! Because Satan remembers us, and he will tempt you again! So beloved, since temptation (sin and Satan) is always at our door, let us exhibit the "upward tendency of righteousness," and pray daily "...lead us not into temptation..." (Luke 11: 4).

God bless you!

Thank You for Praying

"Oh Lord God of my salvation, I have cried day and
night before thee: Let my prayer come before thee:
Incline thine ears unto my cry..." (Psalm 88:1-2)!

We thank the Lord for the people who pray every day. God continue to bless you for your faithfulness! Prayer is the greatest ministry in the world—do not ever be discouraged. There would be no great preachers, missionaries, singers, or churches without great prayer! Jesus bathed His life and ministry in prayer!

Our continuing goal is to:
Inspire deeper relationship with the Lord individually,
Greater unity within the church, and
Greater unity among the churches, and our people, and all we are doing!

Tremendous goals—too much for fallible people? Perhaps! But not too much for God, in Jesus Name! Remember "I can do all things through Christ which strengths me" (Philippians 4:13). And recall what a marvelous thing it is, that we, who feel the weakest, serve a God who bends down His ear from the throne room of Heaven and hears the softest prayer we whisper! Mark 10:46-52 tells us, "Jesus went out of Jericho. Blind Bartimaeus sat by the highway begging. He cried out, 'Jesus, have mercy on me. 'Many charged him to hold his peace. He cried the more, and Jesus stood still! Jesus asked, 'What wilt thou that I should do unto thee? 'He answered, 'Lord that I might receive my sight. 'Jesus said, 'Go thy way, thy faith has made the whole! "Immediately he received his sight!"

If we believe this miracle, why would we doubt that God would withhold our "Prayer Petitions" today? If we will pray about our petitions and believe Jesus!

If we obey Him, and "Let My Prayer Come Before Thee" (Psalm 88:2)!

God bless you!

Thank You Jesus

What is Thanksgiving? It is Joe's thankful testimony! Joe lived in Atlanta Georgia. It was Thanksgiving season, and he was extremely depressed, he was also, unsaved!

He told his friends goodbye, at work and headed home to kill himself! His gun was loaded, and his suicide note written. As he sped around the Atlanta loop, there was a traffic jam, and the loop was shut down. No exit, he was blocked in! Very nervous, he turned on the radio. A religious song was playing!

Joe tried to switch stations, but the dial came off in his hand, fell to the floor and rolled under the seat! Frustrated, he began to weep, and heard the final chorus of the song despite his confusion!

> *"Thank God for the lighthouse, I owe my life to Him,*
> *Jesus is the lighthouse and from the rocks of sin*
> *He has shown a light around me that I could clearly see,*
> *If it were not for the lighthouse, tell me where this ship would be?"[14]*

Joe got out of his car on the roadside, in the traffic jam, knelt and ask Jesus if he could be saved! And he was then and there! Months later, Joe attended a musical concert in his church! Afterward he went up to. Ronny Hinson, writer of that song and testified I do not know you, and you do not know me, but I have met the "Keeper of the lighthouse"! And I am alive, saved, and serving Him!

Beloved, that's Grace! God's "Prayer Grace"! Grace that reaches thru a song, thru a radio, thru a traffic jam and leads a suicide to salvation! So, remember, this thanksgiving season, to pray for all the "Joe's" you know!

God bless you!

---

[14] Ronny Hinson, The Lighthouse 1970, (www.ronnyhinson.com)

The Church Receives Power

"...In the last days, saith God, I will pour out
my Spirit upon all flesh..." (Acts 2:17)

In the early days of America, land west of the Mississippi was known as "The Wild West." Too dangerous to explore; too lawless to settle! But there is a monument that depicts the opposite. It shows a man; his steps pointed westward. Following is his wife. One hand leads a child, her other holds the Bible! The Christian brought the word of God to western settlements; and the church won the west!

Jesus said: "...upon this rock (Peter's confession) I will build my church; and the gates of hell shall not prevail against it" (Matthew 16:18). At Pentecost, the Holy Spirit appeared and empowered the church; "And suddenly there came a sound from heaven as of a rushing mighty wind... there appeared unto them cloven tongues like as of fire, and it sat upon each one of them. They were all filled with the Holy Ghost, and began to speak with other tongues, as the Spirit gave them utterance" (Acts 2:2-4).

What has Christ told us?

First, Christ told those gathered, "...ye shall be baptized with the Holy Ghost, not many days hence." (Acts 1:5) Second, At Pentecost, the Holy Ghost baptized them, and empowered the church. (Acts 2:2-4) Third, God called Ministers (witnesses) for the church (Acts 2:14). Fourth, Christ claimed ownership ("My church") (Matthew 16:18). Fifth, Christ stated the purpose of the church. (Acts 1:8)

These are divine assignments from our Savior: to all people, including you and me! This is a commandment, not an option, it is a personal directive. The Bible states explicitly: "Not forsaking the assembling of we together, as the manner of some is but exhorting one another: and so much more, as you see the day approaching. For if we sin willfully after that we have received the knowledge of the truth, there remains no more sacrifice for sins" (Hebrews 10:25-26).

Be strong, be faithful, be obedient, seek God's will and pray!

God bless you!

The Danger Trail

"For I would that you knew what great conflict
I have for you…" (Colossians 2:1)

This period could be called, "The Danger Trail" of your Christian life! Perhaps we have been saved early, at least in our teenage years. We heard the teaching, preaching, music and prayers inspired by Godly instructors. We learned the Biblical doctrine that solidified our Christian theology. We graduated from high school and moved on to college, employment, marriage, career—whatever life holds for us! You are now in the adult world! "On your own!" "Making your choices!" "The danger trails!"

At this point every born-again believer has great opportunity; yet there is potential danger up ahead. There is temptation, there is sin, there are consequences! The Bible tells us plainly, "For all have sinned…" (Roman 3:23). Yet the scripture promises: We are "justified freely by His grace through the redemption that is in Christ Jesus" (Roman 3:24). The scripture assures us of forgiveness: "There is therefore now no condemnation to them which are in Christ Jesus who walk not after the flesh, but after the spirit. For the law of the spirit of life in Christ Jesus has made me free from the law of sin and death." (Roman 8:1-2)

Whatever our sin, Jesus will forgive us if we repent and pray for His pardon. But we must remain alert. Satan is always near, the Bible says, "…seeking whom he may devour" (I Peter 5:8). This is "the great conflict" that Paul had for the Colossians and we Christians must be aware of! The word he used is "Beware" (Colossians 2:8). We need to remain close to Jesus! The best way is daily Bible study, daily prayer, and regular church attendance.

Keep yourself solid in faith, not in philosophy! Remain steeped in the Word, not in the world! In times like these be especially attentive to your church! Time spent among Christians will strengthen you on your journey along, "The Danger Trail."

God bless you!

The Greatest Ministry

"He gave some prophets; and some evangelists: and some pastors and teachers" Eph.4:11). These are high appointments of God; What about the vast number of Christians who are left out? What is every man to do?

The Bible gives the answer "Prayer!" (1 Thessalonians. 5:17) Each believer; talking with God, listening to God, sharing our deepest thoughts, needs, praise and intercessions with the Father. None are excluded from this (greatest of all ministries). And Psalm 25 is a treasure of thoughts concerning prayer.

I. What does prayer effect?

My soul– The soul is eternal, and the soul is given life at conception, and will live forever. It is this everlasting part of ourselves that we lift-up unto the Lord (Psalms 25 :1).

My will– I live in a world where sin trips me up. When I look to Christ and keep the eyes of my soul, ever toward the Lord, I am delivered time after time.

II. For what shall I pray?

(Psalms 25: 4-22)
Pray for pardon from sin.
Pray for God's direction for your life.
Pray for God's favor and grace.
Pray for deliverance from troubles.
Pray for God's church.

III. What happens through prayer? (Psalms 25:8-14)

Sinners find forgiveness.
The weak and timid are kept safely.
The faithful find favor.

God's peace is extended.
Assurance is the reward of the obedient.

Prayer is the ordained work of every Christian. Prayer is our sword in the battle for the souls of men. Prayer is the light to Christ in a dark world. Prayer may be conducted: in the prison cell, on the sickbed: on the mountain, in the valley; in our strength, and in our weakness, anywhere, anytime throughout life. The ministry of prayer is surely: The greatest of ministries "...for I wait on thee...O God..." (Psalm 25: 21-22).

God bless you!

The Justice of God

"...they are without excuse: because, when they knew God,
they glorified Him not as God." (Roman 1:20-21)

Here is the tragic story of sinful people and the justice of our righteous Heavenly Father. A people who chose to become religiously, morally, and intellectually "perverted." What caused this tragedy?

The Bible says, "...they glorified Him not as God..." (Roman 1:21) They failed to give Him first place in their lives. "There is a way that seems right unto man, but the end thereof are the ways of death" (Proverbs 16:25. And they decided to follow this dangerous path. Question! Is Jesus Christ Lord of your life? Of your present; future; eternity? Of your thoughts; speech; acts? Of your home; work; recreation? God must have total preeminence!

"Neither were (these people) thankful." Their thinking was affected! They became "...vain in their imagination..." (Roman 1:21) they began to take credit for the blessings that God had provided. They turned to self-sufficiency rather than dependence upon God!

"Professing themselves to be wise they became fools" (Roman 1:22). They questioned God! His creation, His word, His existence! Example: During the Second World War, the United States used a small, south sea island as a refueling station for their fighter planes. At war's end they flew the aircraft off the Island: except for one beyond repair. Years later, a group explored the deserted island. They found the abandoned airplane! All vegetation around it was cleared away. Garlands of flowers were draped over the wings. A native tribe was worshiping the airplane. They said it was a chariot in which the Gods flew in and left for them to honor and care for, the myth was that Gods would return!

Ignorance has led to sin of every description: honoring the created above the Creator. So have millions around the earth; many in America!

We must pray daily that our country does not become, slaves of sin (Roman 1:20-32).

God bless you!

The Law Superseded

"For the law was given by Moses, but grace and
truth came by Jesus Christ" (John 1:17).

Here is a doctrine worth remembering! A precept to cherish. There is someone we know who turns failure into faith. One who takes a broken life and by His saving grace, His personal presence, makes the broken, the lost, the forsaken-every bit whole! One who takes the hopeless and restores him to glorify God.

This is the Son of God, who makes the lame to walk, the speechless to talk, and the down-trodden to rise-up and cry out, "Victory!" Beloved, although these are impossible occurrences. They are commonplace happenings in the grace and truth of God! Are you acquainted with this Lord and Savior? "The Divinely Anointed One" – who came to earth to sacrifice Himself and provide us the opportunity of salvation, by believing in Him! God's word is truth. God's grace is His undeserved love. God's salvation is free to all (whosoever); who will pray, repent, confess their sins, ask for His salvation, in Jesus' name. Have you done that?

Oh, I wish I were a, Charles Spurgeon, a Billy Graham, an Apostle Paul— one of those grand orators we read about—not that I might become great, but that I might find a vocabulary that would lead you to pray and believe in Jesus Christ! He said: "I am the way, the truth and the life no man comes to the Father but by Me." (John 14:6)

Deer, friend, prayer, is our contact with God, our heavenly Father! Prayer is our greatest of all ministries! And all people anywhere, anytime, can Pray for forgiveness, for help in a time of need (and for) "…grace and truth which came by Jesus Christ!" (John 1:17)

God bless you!

The Lord's Beauty

"Let the beauty of the Lord our God be upon us..." (Psalm 90:17).

My father had a saying that he shared with his family many times. "Today is bad but tomorrow will be better." Today's text shows that Moses expressed his prayer for God's people in much the same manner! Moses carried a tremendous burden; the welfare of God's chosen! And he began his prayer with praise!

"Lord thou hast been our dwelling place in all generations. Before the mountains...the earth...the world...from everlasting to everlasting thou art God" (Psalm 90:1-2). Moses is quick to acknowledge the omnipotence and limitless knowledge and power of our heavenly Father. Here is the first qualification of every prayer, that we know God is "Almighty," "All Knowing," and "Ever Present"! Anything less would be to give, some-thing else power!

Moses gives all credit for, the days of our years: and our very existence to the will of God. He freely admits the awesome power of God in verse eleven of Psalm 90: "Who knowth the power of thine anger? Even according to thy fear so is thy wrath"!

Having begun with praise and complete dependence toward God, Moses then submits his petition: "Teach us to number our days, that we may apply our hearts unto wisdom. He continues, "...let it repent thee concerning thy servants." He prayed for "...mercy that we may rejoice, (for forgiveness) and be glade all our days" (Psalms 90:12-14.

"Finally (Moses pleads), let thy work (your will) appear, and thy Glory – and the beauty of the Lord be upon us!" (Psalms 90:16-17). Here is the supplication of Moses the man of God. A wonderful example for us to follow. Including: praise, submission, repentance, and forgiveness in our life! Beloved during whatever challenges we face, there is no greater prayer for us to voice:

"Let the beauty of the Lord our God be upon us…" (Psalms 90:17).

God bless you!

The Next Great Awakening

"But ye shall receive power, after that the Holy Ghost is come upon you: And you shall be witnesses unto me both in Jerusalem, and in all Judaea, and unto the uttermost parts of the earth" (Acts 1: 8).

Brothers, and sisters, have you marked the day and the hour? This is such a powerful opportunity for you that love to pray! How long have you been seeking God's face? How many prayers have you sent up to the throne room, beseeching Jesus to honor His people with another "Great Awakening"?

Thousands are bombarding the portals of Heaven, praying for an outpouring of the Holy Spirit. Beloved, if there is to be another in gathering of souls, there must be a beginning somewhere! Would our father allow you and me to experience that time and place? If so, are you willing to include your sacrifice of prayer?

Will you be bold to pull the line which sounds the prayer-bell close to the heart of God? The one that alerts Him to give full attention to the praying saints in God's churches. What are we trying to do, change God's mind? No! Our goal is to find His will concerning a powerful outpouring of His Holy Spirit. Our intent is for many souls to accept Jesus Christ as their Savior! To accomplish this, we must first clean-up our own heart and life. We must follow God's direction not our own. God's will must become our will and prayer will accomplish this!

Take a moment and look up, "The Prayer Revival of 1857-1858" on your computer. See the marvelous work of God recorded there! Sometimes called the "Laymen's Revival," it began with one man praying, and resulted in becoming world- wide! It lasted 50 years, and millions were saved!

Remember: My friend, God can do it! Will you come and help us ask Him?

God bless you!

The Peace of God

"And the peace of God, which passes all understanding, shall keep your hearts and minds through Christ Jesus" (Philippians 4: 7-9).

There is peace to be found in prayer that is unique from any other activity. God intended this to be true, so He listed some thoughts for us to dwell upon in Philippians 4:8-9 these prompt us as we pray, in Jesus' name. Following are some "prayer-thoughts" of my own.

"True"- I think of my salvation. "No condemnation"; "no separation; from Christ." (Romans 8:1, 38- 39)

"Honest"- My mother; at times, more honest than I wanted-but correct, shared in love.

"Just"- My grand-father every word or act; just. most honest man I ever knew.

"Pure"- The laughter of a happy child at play. Pure unrestrained joy.

"Lovely"- The unsolicited approval of a loved one's heart-felt, well done!

"Good Report" - Receiving a good report on a diagnosis of health.

"Virtue"- A long-time friendship that never fades.

"Praise"- Unexpected approval.

These feelings and experiences express my good feelings the best. When I think of them, I am most happy. I feel that things are good between myself, mankind, and God. These are the feelings that I have, "both learned, and heard, and seen." (Philippians 4:9) And when the lessons they have taught me are present in my heart and life, then I am free to pray and know-"the God of peace" (Philippians 4:9).

"Like radiant sunshine that comes after rain, like beautiful rest after sorrow and pain, like hope that is kindled returning again the wonderful peace of my Savior."

"So soft and refreshing as sweet as dew, A promise that cannot be broken to you. A light that will shine the long journey thru Is the wonderful peace of your Savior."[15]

God bless you!

---

[15] Baptist Hymnal, 1956. Alfred Barrett, p.285) Public Domain (www. hymnary.org)

The Power of God

"Finally, my brethren, be strong in the Lord and in
the power of His might" (Ephesians 6:10).

My Christian friend, what does this mean? It means, "faith"! It means, "conviction"! It means, "the perseverance of the saints"! It means, "the security of the believer"! It means, "...as many as received Him (Jesus), to them gave He power to become the sons of God...." (John 1:12) And to those who cannot be shaken, it means, "Once saved always saved"!

Beloved, Christian, Christ has said, "...ye shall have tribulations..." (John 16:33): our faith must always answer as Joshua's did: "...choose you this day whom ye shall serve...as for me and my house, we will serve the Lord." (Joshua 24:15). Your mind must be, made-up now; faith in Jesus Christ must be the strongest strength in your life, today! Is it! The Bible says, "Above all taking the shield of, "faith," wherewith ye shall be able to quench all the fiery darts of the wicked...praying always with all prayer and supplication in the spirit..." (Ephesians 6:16-18)

Perhaps we can out-wrestle a flesh and blood tempter. But a battle with Satan is fighting an invisible adversary, we cannot tell where he will attack next. He has overcome such men as: King David (lust of the flesh); Sampson (lust of the eye); Herod (pride of life). Unless we remain very strong in the Lord, Satan will cause us to spend our life on foolish, useless vanities. Remember when you read the Bible, God is speaking to you, when you are praying you are speaking with God!

Do not waste God's time on frivolous things. In prayer, speak of truth, righteousness, and peace among mankind. Thank your heavenly father for salvation and the blessings of life that you receive. Praise God for friends and family, for the privilege of prayer, the leadership of the Holy Spirit and the forgiveness you obtain in Jesus' name.

Be sure that you, "...be strong in the Lord, and in the power of His might" (Ephesians 6:10).

God bless you!

The Prayer Challenge

"Likewise, the Spirit also helps our infirmities: for we know not what we should pray for as we ought..." (Romans 8:26).

When we pray, God answers our needs! Then we must believe Him explicitly. At times we are very difficult to convince. Our faith is weak, our courage falters, and we miss a great blessing!

Joshua believed and obeyed by faith alone! (Joshua 6:1-21) "...the Lord said...I have given into thine hand Jericho...compass the city once for six days. The seventh day, compass the city seven times... blow the trumpets, ...shout with a great shout, and the walls of the city shall fall..."

An Impossible Battle Plan! What happen? They obeyed God explicitly, by faith, and "they utterly destroyed all that was in the city" (Joshua 6:21).

Gideon obeyed God haltingly, by sight and proof (Judges 6 & 7). The Midianites raided Israel seven years. "...Israel cried (prayed) unto the Lord" (Judges 6:6). God sent an angel to Gideon: "...thou shall save Israel...have not I sent thee (Judge 6:14)? Gideon partly believed! He destroyed the Altar of Baal! Then he called thirty-two thousand men to help him fight. But he needed more assurance, so he: "laid out the fleece."

God said, "Gideon's army, was too large! twenty- two thousands went home. Still too many! God reduced to three hundred. Finally, God sent Gideon to listen to the Midianites fears. They were repeating a dream; they said, "The sword of Gideon" (Judges 7:14).

Finally, Gideon was convinced, and he declared, "Arise, for the Lord hath delivered into your hands the host of the Midian's" (Judges 7: 15)! Each took a pitcher, a lamp, a trumpet, and surrounded the Midianites in the darkness. They broke their pitcher, blew their trumpet, and shouted: "... the sword of the Lord and of Gideon" (7:19-20)!

The Midianites panicked, killing each other and ran! Another Impossible Battle Plan—but it worked! God's plan always works! Some are hard to convince!

My question is how do you pray...like "A Joshua," or like "A Gideon"?

God bless you!

The Spirit Teaches

"...But the spirit itself makes intercession for us with groanings which cannot be uttered!" (Romans 8:26)

Do you pray? Will you pray? If not, why not? We have heard many reasons: "I don't know how, I've just grown cold; A certain thing occurred, and I blamed God; I'm not worthy, I don't have time, I'm living in sin"!

The Bible commands, "Pray without ceasing" (1Thessalonians 5:17.) Not to pray is, sin! And we are persuaded that no Christian can sin successfully, that is, the Holy Spirit will never allow you to be happy in sinfulness. He will accuse you about your sin! It is called, spiritual guilt!

There was no man more determined to stamp out Christianity than Saul of Tarsus! Saul was educated, capable, active, well appointed; but he met Jesus Christ and his life was changed! Now, he is confessing, "...Lord, what wilt thou have me to do..." (Acts 9:6); Now, "...behold, he prayeth" (Acts 9:11), Now, he has a new name, "Paul the Apostle," a new commitment, a new salvation, and a new master, Jesus Christ!

You can too! The same Christ, the same God, and the same Holy Spirit within your life-the same power to guide you, enable you, and prepare you for heaven. When you pray, ask God in Jesus name to save you, and He will! Then the Holy Spirit will take the "things of God" and explain them to you so that what you did not understand, you will. The spirit will open-up the Bible so that you will cherish and love the word. As you speak to the Lord in prayer, your life will become fuller, because you will "...grow in grace and knowledge of our Lord and Savior Jesus Christ" (2 Peter 3:18)!

Every life has a plan and purpose designed by God! Someone said, "Not me, God left me out! I sure wish He would show me." Christ will, if you allow, the Holy Spirt to show you.

God bless you!

The Story of Your Life

"Watch and pray that you enter not into temptation: the spirit indeed is willing, but the flesh is weak." (Matthew 26:41)

What is your legacy? The story of your life! Every person leaves one! We may call it: reputation, habits, impressions, the way we are, temperament; or influence—the things that make us unique. These may be considered good or bad, happy, or angry, helpful, or disturbing, Christian, or not, but they are actions or reactions that express the make-up of our life; they determine our legacy!

My wife's father, a long-time pastor of several churches in Louisiana, raised a family of two boys and seven girls. One of his well-known sayings was, "Don't Miss Heaven." He produced nine praying Christian families and numbers of their offspring. As my wife and I stood at his dying bed, (final conversation) he said to her: "Doris don't miss heaven." Wonderful preacher; dedicated father; yet I remember, him always by those words –what a legacy!

My own mother was the same: praying for me always. Encouraging me to do my best. Advising me with these words: "Stay close to the throne of God." She has been in heaven many years, but her legacy still rings clearly in my mind!

Paul's final words to Timothy (2 Timothy 4:1-8). "I charge thee therefore before God and the Lord Jesus Christ, who shall judge the quick (living) and the dead at His appearing and His kingdom. Preach the (testify) word. ...watch thou in all things—make full proof of your ministry (witness). For I am now ready to be offered and the time of my departure is at hand. I have fought a good (my best) fight, I have finished my course, I have kept the faith: Henceforth there is laid up for me a crown of righteousness, which the Lord, the righteous judge shall give me at that day"!

Beloved, do your best to live and leave a great legacy. You are Important! You will have influence over some. Pray about it every day.

God bless you!

The Tithe

"Bring ye all the tithes into the storehouse, that there may be meat in mine house, and prove me now herewith, saith the Lord of hosts, if I will not open you the windows of heaven and pour you out a blessing, that there shall not be room enough to receive it" (Malachi 3:10).

Far back, God ordained, The Tithe. To be the acceptable measure of wealth that His people should set aside for offerings to Him. (Leviticus 27:30-34) God has not changed His tithe. It is still considered to be ten percent of our time, talent, and treasure. Jesus, speaking of treasures, said: "Lay not up for yourselves treasures upon earth...but lay up for yourselves treasures in heaven...for where your treasure is, there will your heart be also" (Matthew 6;19-21).

Beloved Christian, you may well be a "close-fisted" person with your money in many instances, but you should not hold back in your giving to the kingdom of God! Giving is a commandment not a purpose to ponder about—it is a privilege to obey, and a sin to disobey! For God has decreed: "Bring ye all the (your) tithes... (Malachi 3:10). Here is your opportunity to give of your "first fruits" to your Lord's work for the increase of His gospel.

There is a tremendous benefit to the Christian who obeys. The Bible tells us; "Be not deceived; God is not mocked: for whatsoever a man soweth, that shall he also reap. For he, that sow to the flesh shall of the flesh reap corruption; but he that soweth to the spirit shall of the spirit reap life everlasting. And let us not be weary in well doing; for in due season, we shall reap if we faint not" (Galatians 6:7-9).

My friend, this is the greatest investment in the world. Once begun, the interest is, blessings beyond our ability to receive; backed by God, and the maturity is beyond anything we can imagine "...eye has not seen, nor ear heard, neither have entered into the heart of man, the things which God has prepared for them that love Him" (1 Corinthians 2:9).

If you doubt this, pray! Prayer will convince you.

God bless you!

The Way of the Righteous Shall Prosper

"Blessed is the man (women) that walketh not in
the counsel of the ungodly..." (Psalm 1:1).

The person who delights in God's word, who is sturdy and strong as a well-watered tree, producing fruit. A person who is content within himself. One whose purpose is to be happy with his faith in God, his status in his chosen profession and the talent and treasure God has ordained for him.

I have learned a great lesson! Imagine: at my age-God is still teaching-man (myself) still listening; hopefully! My church held a council meeting this past Sunday. Several members were at this meeting, including myself. Decisions were made, after much discussion concerning the proposed church budget for the new year. We found it necessary to reduce the budget due to the prolonged Covid-19 pandemic which has caused many of our members to stop attending church.

Mostly we were not feeling so happy about this. In closing, our Pastor spoke to our feelings. He reminded us that we were looking at our position from the wrong perspective. We were judging attendance and offerings from where they once had been, judging from the past, waiting for the pandemic to end, and things, meaning attendance and offerings, to return to normal. But this was not going to happen!

Truth is that our church is starting over! With the opportunity of; new converts! new methods! new approaches! not a new gospel! God's word never changes! But a new attitude toward solving our problems. That is really what we need. A new song in our heart; a new lilt to our singing; a new assurance to our prayer life. How about you and yours? Go back and re-read, Psalm One– and find God's blessing for you! Delight yourself in the Lord and what He has done. But lift your mind, your thoughts, and especially your prayers toward the future. Walk in the future; stand upon

God's grace; sit-in the place of progress and bathe each moment in prayer. Be assured; "...whatsoever He (we)doeth) shall prosper...For the Lord knoweth the way of the righteous..." (Psalm 1:3;6).

God bless you!

The Which Way Tree

"Though He slay me, yet will I trust in Him: I will maintain mine own ways before Him. He also shall be my Salvation..." (Job 13:15)!

"Which Way Tree! Texas Revolution (1835-1836)! During the Texas Revolution after the fall of the Alamo, Sam Houston and his army fled to the east from Santa Anna's troops. The road east forked at New Kentucky. One road led to the Trinity and the Sabine River: the other to Harrisburg (known as Houston today). Houston and his men stopped there on April 16, 1836. Near the junction stood a large oak tree with limbs pointing in each direction. One branch pointed northeast to safety beyond the Trinity and the Sabine rivers. The other branch pointed to Harrisburg and to war. As his men took a midday rest beneath that tree, Houston must have considered those roads and reviewed his options. As the story goes, Sam looked at the tree and found his answer. That road led the ragtag little army to victory at San Jacinto just five days (and 18 minutes) later and the Republic of Texas was Born. The oak still stands there today in a small commemorative park, offering respite to modern day picnickers."

"The Which Way Tree" stands in New Kentucky Park at 21710 FM 2920, Hockley, west of Tomball in north Harris County. [16]

There was much praying during this retreat. Many questioned Houston's wisdom. But God heard and answered. While the Texas army rested, Houston stood before the large oak (The Which Way Tree) and received his answer. To the south, Santa Anna's army; to the northeast escape! We believe God answered prayer at that moment: they headed south! Five days later Santa Anna's army was defeated; the Republic of Texas was born!

---

[16] Texas A&M University public Domain (hhttps://tfsweb.tomu.edu/website).

Precious Christian when we pray God hears and answers when we obey. "…All things work together for good to them who are the called (saved) according to His purpose" (Roman 8:28).

God bless you!

The Wonder of Prayer

"Jesus said, arise, and go into the street, which is called
Straight, and enquire in the house of Judas for one called
Saul of Tarsus: for, behold, he prayeth." (Acts 9:11)

We believe, and we testify that Prayer is the greatest ministry in all the world! Prayer enlists the power of God into our life and informs us of God's will! Prayer is our greatest weapon, and our "prayer-closet" is the battlefield. It is here, in prayer, that we engage Satan in spiritual warfare!

Here is the place (Holy Ground) where we de-horn the great serpent– where we pull out the Satan's fangs– where we shut his mouth of blasphemy. (Revelation 13) It is on this battlefield of prayer that we slay the dragon, and send him fleeing away, with the words of our all-powerful Savior, Jesus Christ of God: "...get thee behind me, Satan..." (Matthew 16:23)!

In prayer we draw close to God, and He draws close to us, and the devil is defeated! Prayer is our greatest spiritual weapon! Prayer is our lifeline to Jesus! Prayer is our teacher! Prayer convinces us that:

> *Greatness is found in servanthood!*
> *Success comes through submission!*
> *Power is gained through humility!*
> *Service is our finest activity!*
> *Obedience is our greatest strength!*
> *Holiness is our strongest witness!*
> *Love is our supreme attribute!*
> *Following Jesus, our best ambition!*
> *Prayer is our ultimate conversation!*

"The Priests... arose...their prayer came... even unto Heaven" (2 Chronicles 30:27).

"He will regard the prayer of the destitute..." (Psalm 102:17).

"The prayer of the upright is His (God's) delight" (Proverbs 15:8).

"The prayer of faith shall save the sick..." (James 5:15).

Beloved, the language of prayer is a divine encounter! Speak it often! Speak it gladly! Speak it freely! Speak it reverently; so that you can be sure that, "The words of my mouth, and the meditation of my heart, be acceptable in thy sight, "O Lord My strength, and My Redeemer" (Psalms 19:14).

God bless you!

The Word is, Evangelism

"But watch thou in all things, endure afflictions, do the work of an evangelist, make full proof of thy ministry" (2 Timothy 4:5).

We read this scripture and respond–"Hallelujah"! Evangelism–the theme and thesis of every Christian's calling! The obedience of our greatest purpose! The heart-cry of God's own will!" Jesus has told us: "And this is the Father's will which hath sent me, that of all which he hath given Me I should lose nothing but should raise it up again at the last day" (John 6:39). And Christ reiterates; "...be ye not unwise but, understanding what the will of the Lord is" (Ephesians 5:17).

John expresses God's will best, "...they follow Me; and ...they shall never perish..." (John 10:27-28). The blessed truth that we hold as our infallible promise of God: "once saved, always saved"! How then, can we know this and not make evangelism the joy of our life? This is the greatest story the world will ever know. What could hinder us to pass by unbelievers, the uninformed, and let them continue into a desolate, godless eternity without a word of warning?

When Peter preached his mighty sermon at Pentecost, he ended with "Evangelism;" explaining how the multitude could be redeemed–how they would be saved! Think of your family, your children those looking to you to guide them safely in life, believing in you! Peter said: "...Repent and be baptized every one of you in the name of Jesus Christ for the remission of sins...the promise is to you and your children, and to all that are afar off...as many as the Lord shall call...save yourselves from this untoward generation (Acts 2:38-40).

Nave's Topical Bible describes an "Evangelist" as, "One who preaches (announces) the Good News of Jesus Christ from place to place." Beloved would you become a "Good-News Announcer" and evangelize your family?

Pray and ... "make full proof of your ministry" (2 Timothy 4:5).

God bless you!

This We Know

"And we know that all things work together for good
to them that love God, to them who are the called
according to His purpose" (Roman 8:28).

We know these statements to be factual because we have tested them. And we find that when we obey the word of God, as directed in the Bible, life works out much better for us; when we disobey, we quickly find trouble. This is not to say that we have a perfect life—Jesus said, "These things (commandments) I have spoken unto you that in Me (obeying Jesus) you might have peace. In the world (rejecting Christ) you shall have tribulations; but be of good cheer: I have overcome the world." (John 16:33)

Here is decision time! Also praying time! You probably cannot change your lifestyle, nor your circumstances, but God can, if you want Him to! If you are not a Christian – (1) Pray! Ask God for salvation, in Jesus' name. Then (2) Pray! Ask God to change your lifestyle-He will. (3) Pray! Read the Bible and attend a church. (4) Pray! And allow God to change your life.

> *From troubles to victories; from weakness to strength.*
> *From failure, to winning; from negative, to positive.*
> *From disappointment to happiness!*

Jesus promised: "…I am come that they (meaning you) might have life, and that they (you) might have it more abundantly" (John 10:10). Do this and see–God will not fail you (Roman 8:28)!

God bless you!

Thomas Prayed

"...My Lord and my God" (John 20:28).

Our text: A tremendous example of complete surrender to Jesus! This refers to the Apostle Thomas. When Jesus was told about the illness of Lazarus, He said: "...Lazarus sleepeth (has died); but I go, that I may awake him...." (John 11:11) The Apostles urged Jesus not to go to Lazarus; too dangerous! But Thomas disagreed, "Then said Thomas (which is called Didymus) unto his fellow disciples, let us also go, that we may die with Him (Jesus)" (John 11:16). Thomas, strong and faithful!

Yet, later, they all failed Christ! As the crucifixion drew near, Jesus told Peter: "...before the cock crows twice, thou shalt deny me thrice" (Mark 14:30). Later in Gethsemane, the Bible says, "And they all forsook Him, and fled" (Mark 14:50). Including Thomas! Thomas was told by the other Apostles after Jesus' resurrection, "We have seen the Lord, Thomas replied "...except I see the nail prints in His hands...I will not believe" (John 20:25). Eight days later, Jesus appeared to them, including Thomas, and said, "...reach here... behold my hands...my side...be not faithless but believing" (John 20:27). Then Thomas' great confession and prayer of faith, "...my Lord and my God" (John 20:28). Thomas preached and finally gave his life in India where he was killed by pagan priests, never doubting!

Thomas pictures a great lesson! Today many are half-hearted about Jesus! Is he God 's Son? Did he preform those miracles? Is He really risen from the grave? The answer is, yes! And Like Thomas, we shall everyone see Him! He will come again and judge every person. To the believers He will say, "...Well done thou good and faithful servant... enter the joy of the Lord (eternal life in Heaven)" (Matthew 25:21) To the unbeliever, He will say: "Depart from Me, I never knew you (perdition; Hell)" (Matthew 7:23).

Can you pray, will you pray, right now, even as Thomas did "...my Lord and my God" (John 20:28)!

God bless you!

Those Who Gave

"It is More Blessed to Give Than to Receive" (Acts 20:35).

This is a text for mature Christians! Children and unsaved adults will not agree. Children want all the gifts they can open, and unredeemed adults want worldly things!

We bless the Lord Jesus for coming to save us, and we bless God because, "(He) so loved the world that He gave His only begotten Son, that whosoever believes in Him, should not perish, but have everlasting life" (John 3:16)!

But, although God must give His Only Son, and Jesus must give His life, there were others who gave also, to complete the "Incarnation"! Let us Look at:

Mary - Total obedience! She conceived by a miracle, nurtured, and birthed the Son of God.

Joseph – Accepted extraordinary circumstances. Believed the Angel; married and protected Mary and her divinely conceived child—Jesus Christ.

The Innkeeper – gave the manger for the birth of Christ the Lord.

The Heavenly Angels – First to announce the birth of Christ! "To you is born... a Savior... Christ the Lord" (Luke2:11).

The Shepherds – First to receive Christ's birth announcement, and first visitors!

The Wise men – Traveled a great distance to present kingly gifts, Gold, Frankincense, and Myrrh.

Even a special "Star"! to guide the Wise men to the new-born King.

Christ came to give salvation to all who would believe in Him! The greatest life every lived: A prophet, a priest, a king, but also, a servant, a sacrifice, and a Savior.

The Bible declares: "All things were made by Him; and without Him was not anything made that was made. In Him was life; and the life was the light of men" (John 1:3-4). "He came unto His own... as many as received Him, to those He gave power to become the sons (daughters) of God. Even to them that believe on His name" (John 1: 12). Jesus said: "...It is more blessed to give than to receive" (Acts 20:35)!

God bless you!

Time and Purpose

"To everything there is a season, and a time to every purpose under the heaven" (Ecclesiastes 3:1; 3:17; 8:6).

Beloved, we are famous, for saying, "I just don't have time for – whatever." But we do! Time for the things that are most important to us – the priorities that face us every day. Time to work (money involved); to eat (health involved); to sleep (renewal needed). Anyone will defend these as necessary to the healthy progress of life itself. But are they correct?

What about your soul's salvation? Bible study? Church attendance? Family worship? A witness for Jesus Christ? Prayer? Many people will say: "That's all very well, but my life is too busy; I do not have time." And yet, you do have the time! God speaks very plainly to us all: "...there is a time there for every purpose, and for every work"

(Ecclesiastes 3:17). You have not run out of time; you have run out of purpose! Or you are following the wrong purpose! Dear friend, you would never, intentionally, starve your physical heart, mind, or body.

But by neglecting God's provisions you are doing immortal damage to your spiritual body! You are appointed a specific time to die, physically and that will happen! But spiritually you will never die! You will live on! Where? The most important thing to do, is pray! Get well acquainted with Jesus. Tell Him how you feel. The Holy Spirit will lead you; the Bible says: "If ye be willing and obedient..." (Isaiah 1:19). Brother, you have the time to pray!

If you are an agnostic; non-believer; pagan, or a back-slidden Christian— pray! If you do not know how, speak in your own language—Jesus will hear you! You are that important! I say these things to you because I believe every word of God, and God says, in chapter 12 verse thirteen of

Ecclesiastes: "Let us hear the conclusion of the whole matter: fear God and keep His commandments: for this is the whole duty of man"!

Beloved, there is a time for you!

God bless you!

True Love

"Love not the world...for all that is in the world, the lust
of the flesh, and the lust of the eye, and the pride of life, is
not of the Father, but of the world" (1 John 2:15-16).

Dear friend, there is nothing wrong with having "Things": As long as things do not have you! Then it becomes lust! Some people resemble tyrants due to a promotion on the job!

One of American's wealthy tycoons was asked: Mr. (Tycoon), you have everything. If you could have anything you wished, what would it be? Answer: "Another million dollars"! A second rich man was questioned: Mr. (Rich Man), how much money is enough? Answer: "A little more than you have right now!"—clearly, these men have allowed money to master their lives.

Thankfully, all have not fallen into this "obsession." Many use their blessings to create jobs, fund charities, endow education, and support God's churches. We cannot know the rich person's purposes, but we do know, he cannot buy his soul.

Remember the Rich Young Ruler! He questioned Jesus: "What shall I do that I may inherit eternal life? Jesus answered: Do not commit adultery, do not kill, do not steel, do not bear false witness, defraud not, honor thy father and mother" (Mark 10; 17). I have done that! (Was he feeling pride?). "Then Jesus ...said unto him "...one thing you lackest go thy way sell whatsoever thou hast...give to the poor...take up the cross and follow me" (Mark 10:17-21). The Young Ruler was stunned! The price, too high! The cost too great! The investment too demanding! We know this, because "he went sadly...he went away," (Mark 10:22) But he went! What does the Lord say to you and me?

"Bring ye all the tithes into the store house that there may be meat in mine house and prove me now herewith saith the Lord of host, if I will not open you the windows of Heaven, and pour you out a blessing, that there shall not be room enough to receive it" (Malachi 3:10).

Pray about this-it is a matter of FAITH.

God bless you!

True Repentance

"...be zealous therefore, and repent" (Revelation 3:19).

Beloved I am not a prophet nor a seer of visions; I am a preacher. One who can read the Bible and believe it is infallible. The Scriptures are the words of God speaking to us, individually. They inform us, redeem us, correct us, bless us, and warn us. I submit to you that God is speaking to us through this corona virus.

He is saying: "I know thy works, that thou art neither cold nor hot...As many as I love, I rebuke and chasten: be zealous therefore, and repent" (Revelation 3: 15-19). Recall God's judgment at Mount Sinai...they said to Arron: "Make us Gods...and they offered burnt offerings...they corrupted themselves...the people sat down to eat and to drink and rose up to play... And three thousand men fell that day" (Exodus 32:1-28).

Later: "Israel abode in Shittim and committed whoredom with the daughters of Moab...and bowed down to their Gods" (Numbers 25:1-6). And the people of Baal-Peor were killed. Commandment number six states: "Thou shall not commit adultery" (Exodus 20:14). Yet in so many ways, even today, God's people have turned to sin, and away from God!

Yet, God has sacrificed His Son Jesus, to call men from sin. "John the Baptist came preaching...Repent ye, for the kingdom of heaven is at hand" (Matthew 3:1-2). Luke instructs: "If thy brother trespass against thee...if he repent, forgive him" (Luke 17:3). Peter states: "Repent and be baptized... and receive the gift of the Holy Ghost" (Acts 2:38).

God created every one of us and is continually calling us to repent. Mostly we have turned to pleasures, money, and false Gods. We have found things, that interest us more than God: We are not interested if others are

Christian or not. Is it any wonder that God would possibly use a worldwide virus to show everyone His infinite power?

And say to us: "...be zealous, and repent" (Revelation 3:19).

God bless you!

Trusting in God

"...O God the Lord: In thee is my trust..." (Psalm 141:8).

My preacher father would tell me: "Son, times are hard (and they were) but trust in God, they are going to get better, today's bad but, wait on God!"

Finally, things did improve! After a time, we had food to eat other than red beans. But as we worked, and waited, and prayed, and trusted God—beloved, He made men of conviction, and women of character out of us boys/girls. It was as if we were in a deep valley of life during those 1930's.

But it taught us faith in the Lord and made us "never give up" tough! That is where we are today, in the "school of hard knocks": the valley of Covid-19; the thing that God sometimes allows to attack and teach his children.

I look back and realize that most of the "life lessons" that have sustained me thru the years, are the things I learned down in the "valley of hard-times." We do not learn when things are good in life. On the mountain top of plenty, we spend our time-consuming God's blessings. But when things become difficult; when they remain unpleasant; when no relief is found in about two weeks—we stop and begin to think.

At last, we look up! Finally, we call on God! Then, we are learning to repent and in humility to pray:

"O God the Lord: In thee is my trust..." (Ps. 141:8).

God bless you!

Trusting, Jesus Christ

"...thou art the Christ the Son of the Living God" (Matthew 16:16).

Peter was the first in scripture to make the declaration. It was confirmed many times. Some ninety times in Ezekiel; eighty times in the gospels. Isaiah presented Christ as being called, Immanuel, Mighty God, Everlasting Father, Prince of Peace, Righteous King, Divine Servant, Arm of the Lord, Anointed Preacher, and Mighty Traveler.

Yet there are no words as precious to us as those spoken from Christ's own lips: "...I am the Way, the Truth, and the Life; no man cometh to the Father but by Me" (John 14:6). And none sweeter than these: "Ye have not chosen Me, but I have chosen you; and ordained you...that whatsoever ye shall ask of the Father in My name He may give it to you" (John 15:16).

Still the prayer of Jesus, as He was stripped of His garment and crucified: Even then; publicly humiliated and nailed to the cross, Jesus said: "...Father forgive them; for they know not what they do..." (Luke 23:34). Here is the greatest prayer-words Jesus ever spoke! Deserted and rejected by friends! God the Father turning His face away! Left to carry man's iniquity and pay our unspeakable debt: Him who knew no sin, said: "...Forgive them..." (Luke 23:34)! Greatest act of love in all eternity! He paid it all, that we might live.

Jesus died for all who will believe in Him: because He loved us so! This is His eternal promise to all who will believe Him and pray to accept His salvation:

"Let not your heart be troubled: you believe in God, believe also in Me. In My Father's house are many mansions; If it were not so, I would have told you. I go to prepare a place for you...I will come again and receive you unto myself; that where I am there you may be also" (John

14:1-3). And his greatest promise is "…Because I live, you shall live also" (John14:19).

Dear friend, pray and believe "…Christ, the Son…" (Matthew 16:16)

God bless you!

Under His Wings

"...He shall abide under the shadow of the Almighty" (Psalms 91:1).

God has promised: I may safely trust in Him–if I will abide "...under the shadow...." (Psalm 91:1-4) I saw an example of this in my childhood. I watched a mother hen lead her brood of baby chicks across the front yard. The chicks were scattered around the mother, chirping, learning to peck seeds. Suddenly the mother stopped, spread her wings, gave a "cluck" and eight chicks ran to hide themselves beneath her wings. Looking up, I understood! High above a hawk circled, preparing to dive and pick up one of the chicks. Now they were safely protected, safely under His (her) wings, delivered from the enemy. God had provided for them.

How much greater value are you and me? God also provides for His children: "It was better that a millstone was hanged about his neck, and he cast into the sea, than that he should offend one of these little ones" (Luke 17:2).

Later, the Bible says: "Because Thou hast made the Lord...the Most High thy habitation...There shall no evil befall thee...." (Psalms 91:9-10). God has assigned angels to protect you "...in all thy ways" (Psalms 91:11). This is God's promise to His faithful! This applies to all who follow the Lord's way, and do not deliberately, step outside His will. "The steps of a good man are ordered by the Lord...yet have I not seen the righteous forsaken nor his seed begging bread" (Psalms 37:23-25).

These are the promises of the Lord to the Christian! Not always trouble free; but always blessed and fulfilled! Our Lord declares: "Because He hath set His love upon me, I will... deliver him...set him on high...answer him...-be with him in trouble...deliver him...and honor him. With long life I will satisfy him and show him my salvation" (Psalms 91:14-16).

Pray every day, about everything!

God bless you!

Unity in Prayer

What does this title convey to you? It means, "united"! Togetherness with Christ! Cooperation with others in prayer! There is a hymn that explains the concept more fully:

> *"Nothing between my soul and the Savior,*
> *So that His blessed face may be seen.*
> *Nothing preventing the least of His favor,*
> *Keep the way clear! Let nothing between." [17]*

Do not allow anything you may think or do, disturb the sacred conversation you are having with God, in Jesus' name! That is difficult! But Christ has instructed us explicitly, especially concerning private prayer! This is a conference between yourself and the Almighty, All- knowing, Ever-present, God of heaven and earth! Have we thought of that? You have obtained an audience with Him, through the grace of His Son Jesus Christ. God gives you full attention, give Him complete respect!

Jesus instructs: "…enter into your closet, and when you have shut your door, pray to your Father which is in secret; and your Father which sees in secret; shall reward you openly" (Matthew 6: 6-7). This means you have cleansed you heart and soul of all things displeasing or sinful! Only then are you ready to pray! This confession and forgiveness are required. Why?

The Bible says, "If I regard iniquity in my heart, the Lord will not hear me" (Psalm 66: 18)! Again, (Isaiah 59:2), "But your iniquities have separated between you and your God, and your sins have hid His face from you, that He will not hear"! Now I am prepared, for what shall I pray?

Suggestions:

God's will to be accomplished: In every church, home, and in you!

Thankfulness for His multitude of present blessings!

---

[17] Nothing Between 1905 by *Charles A. Tindley (Hymnary.org)*

Name your sins and blessings (aloud) they become more real.

God's salvation: available to every unsaved person!

That He will guide you in His kingdom's work!

And pray continually:

For this great renewal of prayer, Unity! One in Prayer.

God bless you!

Unknown Seasons

"...It is not for you to know the times or the seasons, which the Father hath put in His own Power" (Acts 1:7).

The followers of Christ Jesus had gathered after the Lord's crucifixion, death, burial, and resurrection, for the purpose of, "what's next?" They were like all of us today– they speculated! And the most impossible and marvelous thing they could ask, "...Lord wilt thou at this time restore again the kingdom to Israel" (Acts 1:6)?

Knowing human nature as we do, it is easy to believe this expectation may have been foremost on their agenda! Why else would He command them to stay in Jerusalem? Had Christ not prepared them for leadership? Given them power; preserved and protected them for the past forty days, surely, they were to be involved in the new kingdom work! And so, they were, but not as they may have surmised!

Jesus answered by giving them "The Great Commission"! "But ye shall receive power, after that the Holy Ghost is come upon you: and you shall be witnesses unto me both in Jerusalem, and in all Judaea, and in Samaria, and to the utmost part of the earth" (Acts 1:8). The promise–"Power"! The command "Witness"! The result—"The World."

They began from there to gather and to pray! On the day of Pentecost their prayers were answered! The Holy Spirit came; filling them with the promised power; gave them the message and the boldness to preach it; and three thousand converts to begin their conquest of the world, in Jesus' name!

The message of Christ has never changed! The Bible is still infallible! The church Christ began will not fail! "...upon this rock I will build my Church; and the gates of Hell shall not prevail against it" (Matthew16:18). Believing, praying Christians are still saved! And Jesus is coming again!

"Jesus Christ... the first begotten of the dead...Him that loved us, and washed us from our sins in His own blood...be glory and dominion forever" (Revelation 1:5-6).

God bless you!

Unlimited Prayer Witness

"...Ye shall receive power..." (Acts 1:8).

How far are your prayers aimed? Jesus is Omnipotent, Almighty- the Holy Spirit, our prayer teacher is unlimited in His world- wide scope, able to reach anywhere, anytime that we voice a petition.

How far did Jesus intend for us to reach when we pray? Acts 1:8 tells us: "...ye shall receive power after that the Holy Ghost is come upon you; and you shall be witnesses unto me both in Jerusalem (your community), in Judea (your State), in Samaria (your Nation), and unto the uttermost parts of the earth (entire World)."

Your prayers are unlimited: and Jesus adds inerrant power: "...lo I am with you always, even unto the ends of the world" (Matthew 28:20). How often have you voiced a prayer for Missionaries? Beloved they are assigned across the world! Separated from home and family, and friends. Many working at secular employment to cover family expenses. And to remain close to the people they witness to. Some are called into places that are very dangerous— so much so, that their location is kept unpublished for fear they might be harmed. Would you pray for these?

We read of one husband and wife. Their mission home is Quebec. There are eight million people who live there also—mostly "French Canadians." The Husband had been there 19 years. Of the eight million citizens in Quebec, about forty thousand are Christians, 0.5 percent! How does anyone stay in these ministries year after year without 'burning out'? It is of because of God's calling, man's surrender, and prayers.

We can be a sustaining force for these who have "left the ninety and nine" and gone alone, "...after that which is lost" (Luke 15:4-7). So, the next time you are in prayer, remember, not only those who are near and dear, but also, those who are far from home and are there in Jesus' name. And do not worry if you do not recall their names, God knows each precious one!

God bless you!

Unseen Love for Jesus

"Whom having not seen, ye love; In whom, though
now ye see Him not, yet believing, ye rejoice with joy
unspeakable and full of glory" (1Peter 1:8).

Much of our praying is spent in asking! For healing; for strength; power; enrichment; advancement or blessings of some kind. We have focused upon the Lord's grace especially in our prayer life. We recall His words and in fact, His emphatic directions concerning prayer: "Ask and it shall be given you; seek, and you shall find; knock, and it shall be opened unto you" (Matthew 7:7).

We are quick to recall this promise and, sometimes, use it as our "never ending shopping list!" Someone asks, is this wrong? And our answer is, no, we have Christ's permission to ask, knock, and seek. But it occurs to our reasoning, what does God think of this pattern, and how glad He might be to hear, at least sometimes, a different motive to our prayers.

God delights to hear from His beloved children. Such as: "...I will behold thy face in righteousness" (Psalms 17:15). Or this, "My lips shall greatly rejoice, when I sing unto Thee..." (Psalms 71:23). Also pray, "...my spirit has rejoiced in God my Savior" (Luke 1:47).

Let our supplication be turned into praise: "I will praise thee with my whole heart–" (Psalm s 138:1); "Praise you the Lord: for it is good to sing praises unto our God: for it is pleasant; and praise is comely" (Psalm 147:1). "...I have found David...a man after my own heart, which shall fulfill all my will" (Acts 13:22).

May our prayers come to God, in Jesus' name, with love, thanksgiving, joy, peace, kindness and assurance-not asking-simply expressing happiness! "... rejoicing with joy unspeakable, full of glory" (1Peter 1:8).

God bless you!

Useless Worry

"Be careful for nothing; but in everything by prayer and supplication with thanksgiving let your requests be made know unto God. And the peace of God, which passes all understanding, shall keep your hearts and mind through Christ Jesus" (Philippians 4: 6-7).

God is either warning us or teaching us! Whichever, he has our attention through this world-wide pandemic, riots, rebellion, and lawlessness. We are persuaded, "God loves us" (I John 4:8). We believe, "All things work together for good, to them that love God..." (Roman 8:28). He knows us personally: The Bible explains explicitly this relationship.

"Whither shall I go from thy Spirit (or) flee from thy presence? If I ascend up into Heaven, thou art there: If I make my bed in Hell, behold, thou art there. If I take the wings of the morning, and dwell in the uttermost parts of the sea; even there shall thy hand lead me, and thy right hand shall hold me. If I say, surely the darkness shall cover me; even the night shall be light about me" (Psalm 139: 7-11).

Then I decide I can pray! Yet the Holy Spirit leads me to Psalm 66:18! "If I regard iniquity in my heart, the Lord will not hear me." And then the Spirit brings to my mind all the thoughts, words, deeds, of which I stand guilty. And I recall: "...The effectual fervent prayer of a righteous man availeth much" (James 5:16). Then I understand! I must pray, first for myself! For my own lifestyle! My conduct! My neglect! God forgive me, for I have sinned!

Brother/sister will you join me in this righteous task? Will you pray for yourself and then for America? Will you join your supplication in this national "prayer chorus," Lord save this land of the free; turn our hearts back to your church, your Bible, your will! Will you forgive us and guide us to re-build the character of our forefathers, whose faith rang out clearly –In God We Trust!

God bless you!

Valley of Dry Bone

"…Son of man can these bones live… O Lord
God, thou knowest" (Ezekiel 37:1-3).

Ezekiel was a priest and prophet to the Israelites taken captive into Babylon by Nebuchadnezzar in 1597 B.C.! Their captivity lasted for seventy years, during which time many became extremely discouraged. But, through Ezekiel (God strengthens) and restored prayer, they were renewed.

God gave Ezekiel a vision! He was transported to a valley filled with human bones, parched and dry, God said "…can these bones live" (Ezekiel 37:3)? There were many bones, and they represented the spiritually dead, hopeless population of God. The Lord instructed Ezekiel, "…prophesy (preach) upon these bones…hear the word of the Lord…I will cause breath to enter into you, and you shall live… I will lay sinews upon you and will bring flesh upon you and cover you with skin and put breath in you, and you shall know that I am the Lord" (Ezekiel 37:4-6).

As Ezekiel preached, the long-dead bones revived, renewed, breathed again, "…and stood upon their feet, an exceeding great army…the whole house of Israel" (Ezekiel 37:10-11). These were they, like us today and so many around the world, who have given up hope that we will return to normal again! Sadly, some think that God is not able to bring order to the sickness, lawlessness; physical, mental, emotional, and spiritual chaos that has gripped our nation! Many have almost lost faith; others have no faith at all! But my friend, you are wrong! Jesus commanded all of us: "…Have faith in God" (Mark 11:22).

Your answer is prayer! Talk to God; ask Him to help you; ask Him, in the name of Jesus Christ. If you have never been saved, ask Him to forgive you and change your spiritual heart. It is called "repentance." It means you have changed your way of thinking, and Jesus, will change your heart.

That is what God did for the spiritually dead Jews over there in Babylon. And God, in Jesus' name, can do this for you!

God bless you!

Waiting Patiently

"But there is forgiveness with thee—" (Psalm 130:4).

Recall singing: "I will watch, I will pray, I will labor every day...in the vineyard, in the vineyard of the Lord." Really? Are we doing that? Are we faithful in daily prayer? In Bible study? In church attendance? Faithful to obey?

We believe that God, "your Father knoweth what things ye have need of" (Matthew 6:8). He urges us to wait patiently for His answer. Many try, few succeed! We are created in god's image but mostly we forget; we substitute our persona for God's image especially when we get in a tight spot! Like we are right now: The "corona virus" is upon us! We never dreamed it would get this bad or reach this far! World-wide!

Does God not know we are in desperate straits? Of course, he does. Then what is His purpose? Brother/sister, He is speaking to all the people. How better to get our attention? When every Doctor has failed, God says: "...humble themselves and pray, and seek my face, and turn from their wicked ways...then will hear... forgive...and heal..." (2 Chronicles 7:14). Remember, God is still in heaven: we are still on earth! He warned early in our history: "...My spirit will not always strive with man" (Geneses 6:3).

Humanity has ignored this; has overstepped himself, and our Father has said: Enough! Let us bow down ourselves; lift obedience to our Father; repent in Jesus' name, and pray as Daniel did in Babylon: "O my God... not for our righteousness, but for thy great mercies; O Lord, hear; O Lord forgive; O Lord hearken and do; defer not, for thine own sake, O my God: for thy city (world) and for thy people called by thy name" (Daniel 9:18-19).

Beloved, pray to the One, who can heal.

God bless you!

War Council

"By wise counsel thou shall make thy war" (Proverbs 24:6).

There is a time when Christians are called upon to fight! When God's Word, Your Family, Christianity is in jeopardy. However, it is a Christian's last resort. And surely it depends upon the circumstance. Today the world is engaged in a war such as we have not witnessed; It is named "Corona Virus"! No treatment, no cure, thus far a war that attacks without warning and takes health and lives!

This terrible illness of unseen, unknown origin has devastated our world and confused our learned experts. Father, we have not seen an enemy like this. We have not known a worldwide epidemic before. Therefore, we cry out to you Lord is this your hand of judgement upon all people. Is this a reminder that you have said, "The wage of sin is death..." (Roman 6:23)! And have we turned from you as others whom you spoke of: "... The people sat down to eat and drink and rose up to play" (1 Corinthians 10:7).

Lord we remember many times: your people have placed sin above your righteousness, and man's ways before your ways. But we remember each time your hand of judgement fell upon the people–yet when they repented and turned back to you, –you were merciful and forgave their iniquities. We know we are sinful people, help us to confess and pray; To ask your forgiveness and renew our vows of righteousness. Cause, "In God we trust" to become stamped in our hearts once more! Let us be, "One nation under God" is our promise and "...peace good will toward men" (Luke 2:14). becomes the truth that unites us!

Father guide us back to your church! Lead us to your prayer altar! Break our hearts before your presence! Have mercy upon our people! Convict us of the truth,

"...In multitude of counsellors (In prayer) there is safety" (Proverbs 24:6).

God bless you!

With All Your Heart

"You shall seek me, and find me, when you
search for me..." (Jeremiah 29:13).

The song asks, "Are you weary, are you heavy hearted. Tell it to Jesus, tell it to Jesus" (In prayer) (Matthew 11:28). A modern version inquires: Have you talked to the man upstairs? He wants to hear from you!

Today's complaint is, "I am absolutely stressed out!" About my marriage, my money, my employment, illness, failure, my temper, loss, etc. "Stress" can mount about most anything, and Satan is an expert at using our emotions against us: stress tends to affect us negativity! We fail to realize; negativity leads us to a short temper: undue anger which changes our personality. Friends stop speaking; groups do not include us as they once did; finally, we do not enjoy anything or anyone!

What has happened? What is wrong with me? The answer, stress has led me into a serious state of depression! And prolonged depression can destroy a person! I need to do a personal introspection! God has created within us the ability to step outside and look at ourselves. Animals cannot do this - we can!

Be honest! Look inside your spiritual heart! God the Holy Spirit will help you– if you ask Him! Jesus said: "But seek ye first the kingdom of God, and His righteousness: And all these things shall be added unto you" (Mathew 6:33). If you are not saved: Ask God, in Jesus' name, to forgive your sins and save your soul! Then ask for the help you need.

If you are God's child, tell Him your problem! And make no mistake; have no doubt; God in Jesus' name, is your answer! He, and He alone can lift any burden, solve any problem, and relieve any stress that is destroying your peace of mind. And when your prayer is answered, do not forget to thank Him. You found your answer:

"When ye seek Me… and when searched for Me with all your heart" (Jeremiah 29:13).

God bless you!

With Prayer and Thanksgiving

"I will bless the Lord at all times. His praise (my prayer)
shall continually be in my mouth." (Psalm 34:1)

Give yourself to prayer, and get your texts, your thoughts, your words from God. Martin Luther spent his best three hours every morning in prayer. (Robert Murray McChesney) and this great preacher was correct in doing so. There is infinite power in prayer. God's message to humanity is imparted through earnest time in prayer. Our Heavenly Father opened this marvelous miracle of communication between mankind and Himself so that we may speak with Him at any time.

The Bible indicates that the exercise of praying began far back, in the day of Adam's grandson, Enos. "And to Seth was born a son; and he called his name Enos: then began men to call on the name of the Lord" (Genesis 4:26). The Christian who deliberately reads the Bible will understand the saving grace of God if he humbles himself in regular prayer.

Also, there is a blessed comfort in prayer. Comfort even in our prayer-closet. Because we are not alone; the Holy Spirit is present to assist you as you pray, and Jesus is there to receive your needs and wishes as you speak, them in His name. There is a peace of mind that, the Bible says, is beyond our understanding. As you unburden your soul, "...the Spirit also helps our infirmities: for we know not what we should pray for as we ought..." (Roman 8:26). Our Lord comforts us in all ways when we have audience with Him.

Greatest of all we please God when we obey His word and call on Him in prayer. For so has He commanded us to do: "...in everything by prayer and supplication with thanksgiving let your requests be made known unto God" (Philippians 4:6).

Not only these blessings, but we have the benefit of telling Jesus the most private things of our live: hurts and anxieties to sharp too private, to share with anyone else, can be shared in the solitude of prayer.

"In Thee, O Lord, do I put my trust..." (Psalm 71:1).

God bless you!

Witness, He lives

"And the Word was made flesh, and dwelt among us..." (John 1:14)

"In the beginning God created the heaven and the earth" (Genesis 1:1). "But when the fullness of the time was come, God sent forth His Son, made of a woman... made under the law, that we might receive the adoption of sons" (Galatians 4:4-5). Christ taught the truth about sin and salvation: "He that believes on the Son has everlasting life; and he that believes not the Son shall not see life..." (John 3:36).

Jesus Christ died for our sins: they crucified Him, and Jesus prayed, "... Father forgive them; for they know not what they do..." (Luke 23:34). Christ rose from the dead: "The angel said—I know that you seek Jesus, which was crucified. He is not here: for He is risen, as He said. Come see the place where the Lord lay" (Matthew 28:5-6).

We have Biblical record that Christ appeared alive forty days: teaching and proving His resurrection! 1. He appeared to Mary Magdalene (Matthew 16:9). 2. Then to the other women (Matthew 28:9). 3. To Peter (1 Corinthians 15:5). 4. Two disciples (Luke 24:150. 5. Ten apostles (John 20: 19 & 24). 6. Eleven Apostles (John 20:26&28) 7. Seven disciples (John 21:1-24). 8. Jesus' charge to Peter (John 21:15-17) 9. To five hundred (1 Corinthians 15:6). 10. To James (1Corinthians 15:7). 11. At His ascension (Acts 1:2-9). 12. Twice to the Apostle Paul/Saul (Acts 9:1-5 & 1 Corinthians 15:8).

Then Jesus instructed: "...ye shall receive power after that the Holy Ghost is come upon you, and you shall be witnesses unto Me: in Jerusalem; Judaea; Samaria; and (all) the earth" (Acts 1:8).

Beloved, that is our privilege and assignment! Our directives come through the Bible and prayer! God will hear, answer, direct, and teach us, as we pray! Take the time, make arrangement, join us as we pray.

God bless you!

You are Commanded and Empowered

"…ye shall be witnesses unto Me…" (Acts 1:8).

Prayer and Evangelism are always welded together. A Christian gentleman said to me: "I cannot find a ministry, what can I do?" My answer, pray first, and listen to Jesus' instructions.

"You shall receive power, after that the Holy Ghost is come upon you: And you shall be witnesses unto me both in Jerusalem (your community) and in all Judaea (your state) and in Samaria (your America) and unto the uttermost parts of the earth (your world) (Acts 1:8).

Beloved, how are you doing with this Scripture? It is a commandment not an option! I had a couple whom my wife and I were visiting, tell me about their church attendance, the wife said: "We know we ought to go, but since we moved, we just haven't found any place to attend". To my recollection, they moved to their new location about fifteen years ago! Wasted years!

Jesus also said, "…Thus it is written, and thus it behooved Christ to suffer, and to rise from the dead the third day. And that repentance and remission of sins should be preached in His name among all nations, beginning at Jerusalem (where you are), and you are witnesses of these things" (Luke 24:46-48). The question is, do we know these things? Of course, we do! Are we obedient– kind of? At times? Sometimes? Never? We must answer the question for ourselves!

One thing we can be sure of: If we pray and witness, some will respond! Some will visit our church! Some will be saved! We are not accountable for someone's decision; that is the work of God the Holy Spirit! Not for a person's salvation, which is the redeeming work of God the Son, Jesus Christ!

We are responsible to pray for and wittiness to whomever and whenever we have opportunity! "…both in Jerusalem, Judaea, Samaria, and the uttermost parts of the earth" (Acts 1:8) Jesus did not ask, He commanded and empower us! Whatever you do please make prayer the priority of your life! It is serious business. The Bible contends, to neglect prayer is a sin!

God bless you!

Printed in the United States
by Baker & Taylor Publisher Services